Dealing in Votes

*Interactions between politicians and
voters in Britain and the USA*

IAIN McLEAN

Martin Robertson · Oxford

© Iain McLean, 1982

First published in 1982 by
Martin Robertson & Company Ltd.,
108 Cowley Road, Oxford OX4 1JF.

British Library Cataloguing in Publication Data
McLean, Iain
    Dealing in votes.
    1. Elections—Great Britain 2. Elections—
    United States
    I. Title
    324.2'1   JN1001

    ISBN 0-85520-472-9
    ISBN 0-85520-473-7 Pbk

Typeset in 10 on 12 pt Vladimir
by Pioneer Associates, East Sussex.

Printed and bound in Great Britain by
Billings, Worcester

For RCB, JP, SJP.

Contents

Acknowledgements

Much of this book was drafted in the autumn of 1980 while I watched the US election from the attractive vantage point of Lexington, Virginia. My first debts are to my college for giving me leave, and to Washington and Lee University for an extremely warm reception, an excellent working environment and a most useful library.

I should like to thank all the colleagues who commented helpfully on draft chapters: in the USA 'Buck' Buchanan, Philip Converse, John Handelman, Gordon Tullock and Spencer Wellhofer, and in the UK David Austen-Smith, Hugh Berrington, David Earnshaw, Adrian Ellis, Jonathan Hourigan, Philip Norton, Derek Parfit, Jo Poulton, Andrew Reeve and Alan Ware. Janie Hughes, Betty Donaghy and Elizabeth Bowles all struggled with my handwriting and won.

I am especially grateful to the practising politicians and civil servants who took time to answer my questions and to comment on parts of the book. I must also record my debt to the electors of St. Antony's, Newcastle-upon-Tyne, and my colleagues on Tyne and Wear County Council for six years of intensive political education.

I have learnt a lot from my students in two British and two American universities. In particular, they have helped me to see each political system through the eyes of somebody accustomed to the other one and taught me which are the important questions to ask.

Intellectual debts are not simply measured by square-footage of references. I owe special thanks to Philip Williams, who first taught me how to assess evidence and set it out coherently, to Hugh Berrington for eventually persuading me that there is more to political psychology than Freudian mumbo-jumbo, and to David Soskice and the late John Mackie for general and particular intellectual

stimulation. Literary detectives may spy Oxford bits, Newcastle
bits, Virginia Polytechnic bits; it goes without saying that nobody
who works at any of these institutions, nor anyone else mentioned
in these acknowledgements, bears any responsibility for the contents
of this book.

Writing books is a strenuous and can be a lonely occupation. A
lot of people helped me remain sane which I was writing this one.
My friends and colleagues in all sorts of organisations from the
Welshpool and Llanfair Light Railway to the Washington and Lee
rugby team helped to take my mind off it when that was most
needed. Three people helped above all. There is no direct reference
to them in what follows; but I could not have written this book
without them. I dedicate it to all of them with affection.

Iain McLean
Oxford
1981

Introduction

This is partly a book about voters and partly a book about politicians. But, more than either of these things, it is a book about the *interactions* between them: about what the people want, how they convey their wishes to politicians, and what the politicians do about them. This covers a multitude of actions and omissions. Citizens may vote for one or another party, or abstain from voting. They can become active in a party and try to change its policies. They can demonstrate in the streets. They can join a revolutionary conspiracy and try to overthrow the government by force. They can join groups which put pressure on the government to make changes. Or they can be 'free riders' who reap any benefits 'their' group produces without contributing to the costs it incurs. They may strike for more than their government's wages policy would allow them to get. They may invest their capital (if they have any) overseas instead of at home. Many of them (between thirty and forty per cent of the workforce in Britain, for instance) get their wages more or less directly from the government, because they work for it, or for local government, or for a state-owned trading enterprise. These people have an interest in bargaining direct with the government, over and above their interests as citizens. Teachers have an interest in the welfare of children; they also have an interest in the welfare of teachers. People whose job is to implement government policy have yet another set of interests. A civil servant is paid to carry out the policy of the government of the day; he also has an interest in policies which promote the welfare of civil servants.

This list of actions, choices and motives is wide-ranging but not comprehensive. It covers only a small fraction of the political activities a citizen can undertake. Every action designed to influence the policy of the government, or of a possible future government, is a political action. And there is an even larger class of actions which

1

influence governments without being specifically designed to do so. People form a pressure group to lobby for subsidies for the local railway line: a deliberate political action. At the same time, they are choosing to use their cars instead of the train: not a deliberately political action, but equally one which the government ought to take into account when it decides what to do. Each part of this book will examine one element of these interactions. Part I deals with one specific sort of activity: voting. Part II takes on the task of exploring some things other than voting which citizens do when they want to influence their government: joining pressure groups, for instance, or becoming party activists. Part III deals with politicians' responses: why do they deliver the policies they do? Why do they play the game at all? After all, only a quarter or at most a half of adult citizens abstain from voting, but over 99 per cent of them abstain from being politicians. In trying to answer all these questions, we shall stray into a wide range of academic disciplines. None of them has a monopoly of wisdom.

Part I

The Voters

What is so special about voting? Why single it out for a section of the book on its own, and the first section at that? There are two reasons, one grander than the other. The first is that the chance to cast an uncoerced vote is the one thing that infallibly distinguishes a democracy from any other sort of régime. Every régime has *some* interaction between its citizens and its government. As David Hume pointed out two centuries ago, even the most despotic tyrant must at least make sure he pays attention to the wishes of his palace guards. But in democracies, and only in democracies, politicians derive their right to rule from the fact that more people voted for them than for any of the other teams on offer. The unique importance of voting was obvious enough to campaigners for votes for women in the Britain of 1910 or for blacks in the USA of 1954: students sometimes lose sight of it now, but they shouldn't.

The less grand fact about votes in free elections is that they can be accurately measured. Nobody will ever know *exactly* how much influence the British Medical Association had on the final shape of the National Health Service legislation in 1948. But anybody who looks it up can find out that the Labour Party got 11,632,891 votes in the General Election of 1945. That is one reason why many of the first scientific studies of politics concentrate on voting.

The first part of this book is intended to introduce students to these studies. Chapter 1 looks at three different ways of studying voting. Chapters 2 and 3 record what the studies have told us about the British and the American voter. Chapter 4 explores one of the methods — the formal, deductive, one — in greater detail.

Part I

The Voices

1

Voting: three approaches

They employed, indeed, for the most part, different materials; but as
the materials of both were real observations, the genuine product of
experience — the results will in the end be found not hostile, but
supplementary, to one another.

J. S. Mill (1840) on Bentham and Coleridge

ELECTORAL GEOGRAPHY

The first scholars to study elections scientifically were geographers.
Indeed, the earliest and one of the best (Siegfried 1913) might even
be described as an electoral geologist. The north-west of France,
which Siegfried studied, was one of many rural areas where political
allegiances went back for generations, even beyond living memory.
If one village voted for the secular parties and the next one voted for
the Catholic parties in 1913, the chances were that in 1789 the first
had been for the Revolution and the second had been for King
Louis XVI.

Siegfried managed to show how differences in voting were related
to different forms of land tenure, different sizes of holding, and
different crops. All of these gave people diverse, and often
conflicting, economic interests; and these facts of economic
geography could be traced all the way back to geology. In the
Vendée region for instance, villages in the 'ancient landscapes and
woodlands' voted for the right-wing parties, and those in the
'calcareous and Quaternary regions' voted for the left-wing parties.
In the département of the Eure, around the town of Evreux, the
apple-growing areas were Bonapartist and the cereal-growing areas
were leftist (Siegfried 1913, pp. 11, 34-5, 277-9).

Siegfried's analysis was geological not only in the literal sense,
but in the sense that it showed that some very profound continuities
underlay voting behaviour — continuities often dating back to

5

a time before most people had the vote. Electoral geography has not been much studied in either Britain or the USA. That is a pity, because some patterns of behaviour in both countries have very ancient origins. The British Conservative Party is generally strong rurally, but there are three areas where it is relatively weak: the Highlands of Scotland, rural Wales and Devon and Cornwall.[1] The explanation for this may be literally geological (they are all areas of ancient rock, which produces mountainous terrain and poor, acid soil; many poor farmers cultivate it and a few rich sportsmen shoot over it; the poor farmers support whatever party or parties oppose the party of the rich sportsmen). It may also be geological (glaciological?) in the second sense. In Caithness and Sutherland, the Conservative agent once told the author that the local weakness of the Conservatives was due to the Sutherland Clearances — the eviction of crofters from their smallholdings by the Duke of Sutherland's land agent between 1817 and 1822.

Even without going so far back in picturesque detail, some British and American studies of electoral geography can tell us a lot about stable voting patterns. We shall look at two important studies: Pelling's *Social Geography of British Elections* (1967), and Lipset's *'The Election of 1860 and the emergence of the one-party South'* (1960, Ch. 11).

The eight British general elections between 1885 and 1910 were all fought on the same franchise and the same boundaries. They can therefore be read as a series, where one can look for long-run patterns and continuities not obscured by the upsets of one particular election. Pelling (1967, p. 415; cf. also Bealey and Pelling 1958, ch. 1) used this series to show that there were three main factors at work in voting behaviour. One was class. The fifty-six constituencies with at least one female domestic servant to every four households formed the most Conservative of any group that Pelling described: the fifteen seats in England with the highest numbers of coal-miners formed one of the most anti-Conservative. But the influence of class was crosscut by those of region and religion. Broadly speaking, the further a constituency was from London, the less likely it was to support the Conservatives. The principal exception — Protestant areas of Ulster — occurred because the politics of religion mattered much more to Ulstermen than the politics of region (they still do). The regional voting patterns showed that the Conservatives were very much the party of the geographical core, physically and socially close to London. They were the party of what has been called the 'nation-building' élite. Their Liberal, Labour, and Irish Nationalist opponents were the parties of the 'subject-periphery', which resented and resisted the spread of central control over their affairs.

This is not just a historical curiosity. Of the three bases of political alignment which existed between 1885 and 1910, religion has almost (not quite) disappeared: the number of actively religious citizens has declined, and the proportion who take their religious concerns into politics has declined still more. Class, of course, has grown greatly in salience. But centre-versus-periphery never disappeared, and since the early 1960s it has revived quite sharply. Two examples are the rise of the Scottish Nationalists and the 'North and South' election of 1979, at which Conservative support in all social classes increased steadily the nearer a constituency was to London.[2]

Pelling's work on British electoral geography, like Siegfried's on France and Key's (Key 1949) on the US South, was a labour of love. All involved their authors in many years' collection of curious and apparently disconnected facts. They owe a lot of their quirky fascination to the apparently useless facts they skilfully muster, about apple-growing in Evreux and bribery in Maidstone and the MP who donated a public park to every town in the Wick Burghs constituency. It is not surprising that none of them has been followed up. Indeed, they share some serious problems of method, to be discussed in detail later, which would make any follow-up tricky.[3]

The problems of method can be sidestepped by using opinion surveys rather than election results. But survey research dates back only to the 1930s. Almost every attempt to find out what earlier generations of voters were up to has to rely on electoral geography — or indeed geology. A well-known exposed stratum is the behaviour of voters in the Southern states of the USA. As everybody knows, the South has traditionally supported the Democratic party, the more left-wing of the two American parties and the one supported by most low-status people. This immediately poses two problems. Why should upper-class Southerners have pitched their lot in with a mainly lower-class party? And why should a group who favoured white supremacy and opposed civil rights for black Americans join a party which contains the leading actors on the other side? Part of

the answer lies in the concept of 'party' itself, which is much looser
in the USA than in Britain. Anybody who wishes to call himself a
Democrat can do so, and nobody can stop him from running under
that title, whatever his ideological views; and if politicians from the
South run for the US Congress as Democrats rather than
Republicans, they have for many years stood to gain clear
advantages of seniority and majority status. But this begs the
question of how the South came to be Democratic in the first place.
The answer is historical. Abraham Lincoln freed the slaves and
ended the secession of the Confederate States; Abraham Lincoln
was a Republican; therefore the white citizens of the old Confederacy
vote Democrat. But there is more to it than that, as Lipset's
pioneering analysis showed. His method was to study voting in
1860 and 1861 in Southern counties for which statistics were
available, dividing them into counties with a high, medium and low
slave population. He postulated that the high-slave areas were
dominated by rich plantation owners and the low-slave areas by
relatively poor white farmers with few or no slaves.

The presidential election of 1860 was a four-way fight. The
Democratic party had emerged during the Presidency of Andrew
Jackson (1829-37) as the party of low-status, mostly rural,
Americans, who were deeply suspicious of the rich, the educated,
the North-east, and any interference in their affairs by the Federal
government. The Kentuckian Jackson was the first frontiersman to
become President, the first who conspicuously rejected eastern
values both in what he said and what he did. By 1860, however, the
Democratic party could no longer agree on the South's 'peculiar
institution' — slavery, and particularly on whether slavery could be
permitted in the new territories being colonised as the USA expanded
westwards. The party split, with the northern wing nominating
Stephen Douglas and the southern wing John C. Breckinridge. No
corresponding party had united high-status Americans. But some of
them in the North had deserted the old Whig party in favour of a
new, more pronouncedly anti-slavery, party called the Republican
party. Formed in 1854, it nominated Abraham Lincoln for President
in 1860. Lincoln did not get a single vote in the deep South. The
candidate of the upper-class Southerners was John Bell, who wished
to preserve both the Union and the 'peculiar institution'.

Lincoln won the election, though with only 39.9 per cent of the
vote.[4] Lipset shows that the Southern vote probably split along

class lines. The counties with fewest slaves (and hence, presumably, the most poor whites) voted most heavily for Breckinridge. The South was not a one-party state in the election of 1860; it divided along class lines much as most of Britain and the USA do at the moment. It was the election of Lincoln that changed everything. Of the candidates, Lincoln was the most determined upholder of the Union, and the South also thought (quite wrongly) that he would immediately try to abolish slavery. Secessionist feelings grew fast, and within a few months most southern states held referenda to decide whether to secede from the Union. A remarkable reversal of the 1860 result took place. Counties with a high proportion of slaves voted *for* secession, where in 1860 they had voted for unionist candidates (Bell or Douglas); those with a low proportion of slaves voted *against,* though many of them had voted for a secessionist candidate (Breckinridge). Does this mean that the slave owners voted unionist in 1860 and secessionist in 1861, while the poor whites voted secessionist in 1860 and unionist in 1861? Lipset says it does, but his data (Table 1.1) actually show something subtler.

Readers with a phobia for figures should not despair; the message is not too hard to read. Although high-slave counties voted for secession by 130 to 51, those of them which had supported Breckinridge were more secessionist than those which had not. The same pattern appears in the medium and low-slave counties. At each level of slave ownership, counties which voted Breckinridge in 1860 were more likely to vote for secession in 1861 than counties which did not. Probably, therefore, the strongest backers of secession were poor whites *in slave areas.* But many slave owners obviously moved into the secessionist, and hence Democratic, camp because only the (southern) Democratic party unequivocally supported both slavery and secession. And there they remained for over a century.

The great virtue of an analysis like Lipset's is that, by bringing the voters of 1860 back to life, it fills in the necessary historical perspective without which the impression of Southern voting would be flat and inexplicable. But it is instructive only in describing a stable electorate; it cannot help if the social composition of the electorate changes rapidly or extensively. Politics in Earls Court now is not like politics in Earls Court in 1914. Politics in the Deep South in the 1950s was still recognisably like politics there in the 1860s, but it has now changed fundamentally because the blacks,

TABLE 1.1

RELATIONSHIP BETWEEN 1860 PRESIDENTIAL VOTE AND 1861 REFERENDUM VOTE IN 537 SOUTHERN COUNTIES

Presidential vote, 1860:	Proportion of slaves in county							
	High				Medium			
	Breckinridge		Bell/Douglas		Breckinridge		Bell/Douglas	
Referendum vote, 1861:	n	%	n	%	n	%	n	%
Secession	77	82	53	61	71	82	20	30
Union	17	18	34	39	16	18	46	70
	94	100	87	100	87	100	66	100

Presidential vote, 1860:	Low				Total	
	Breckinridge		Bell/Douglas			
Referendum vote, 1861:	n	%	n	%	n	
Secession	65	50	10	14	296	
Union	65	50	63	86	241	
	130	100	73	100		

Source: Lipset 1960, Table III on p. 350. Source gives percentage figures and column total *n*s only.

nominally enfranchised after the Civil War, actually got the vote only from the 1950s onwards. The parts of the Deep South which are still solidly Democratic are so for largely different reasons than in 1861 or 1952.[5]

The even deeper problem with the geographical approach is known as the 'ecological fallacy', and it is so pervasive that Lipset, who warned his readers solemnly against its dangers (p. 351), did not notice that he had just committed an example. The data we have discussed so far are about groups, not individuals. We know how constituencies in Britain, villages in France, and counties in the USA voted. We can compare their votes with other statistics we have about the number of miners in the constituency or of apple-trees in the village or of slaves in the county. We can note correlations: the more miners in the constituency, the more likely it was to return a Liberal or Labour MP. What we cannot legitimately do is take the apparently obvious next step, 'Therefore the miners voted Liberal or Labour'. The truth may be quite different. Perhaps it is that all farmworkers vote Tory, all clog-makers vote Liberal, and no miners vote at all. Constituencies with unusually many miners also have unusually many people making clogs for them, and unusually few farmworkers (because all the farmland either has pit-heaps on top of it or has had its drainage ruined). There is a correlation between proportion of miners and Liberal voting, but a correlation is not an explanation.

Of course, my counter-example is absurd. Everybody knows that miners did indeed vote Liberal or Labour. There is plenty of other evidence for that. And there is no harm in saying that the most plausible (in this case, the only plausible) explanation of the correlation between number of miners and left-wing voting is that the miners voted for the left-wing parties. But often the immediate explanation is not the true one, and it is very easy to get trapped as Lipset does. And legions of writers about bygone elections have ridden into the trap with all banners flying, often unaware that it was there at all. One way to avoid it is never to make any speculations about individuals unless we have data about individuals. But this is too austere and restrictive. Used with caution, the information presented by scholars like Siegfried, Lipset, Key and Pelling can illuminate murky corners of electoral history.

The other way to avoid the trap is to use such information about individuals as does exit. For Britain, pollbooks are an important and still under-used source. Up to 1872, the vote was not secret, and local booksellers or journalists sometimes compiled lists, known as pollbooks, showing how everyone in the constituency had voted. The most useful pollbooks show voters' occupations as well as their names. In Bristol, in 1852, fifty-six out of the fifty-nine Anglican clergymen (together with all the sextons, organists and gravediggers) voted Tory, and every Nonconformist minister except one voted Liberal (Vincent 1967, p. 85.). That does not leave much room for doubt that religion played an important part in determining people's voting behaviour.

THE SURVEY APPROACH

But pollbooks came to an end with the secret ballot in 1872. Since then, there has been no official or semi-official information about how individuals voted. Indeed, British law is so keen to preserve the secrecy of individual ballots that, unlike American or French law, it forbids the publication of electoral data for any level below the unit of election: in other words, parliamentary results are given only at the constituency level and local results only at the ward level. The results from precincts or individual ballot boxes are not reported, as they are in most democracies; in fact, the papers from all the ballot boxes must by law be shuffled together before counting starts, in case any party agent at the count should get an illicit impression of how Commercial Road voted. So the only reliable way of finding out how individuals voted (or didn't vote) is to ask some of them. Providing they are selected in a systematic way, the information they provide may be generalised to cover the population from which they have been sampled. This has been the basis of all good survey research since it began in the 1930s. Details of what it can tell us about British and American voters are in the next two chapters. The rest of this section explores what survey research can and cannot do in principle.

Opinion polls do not have a very good name, especially among politicians. There are many common criticisms of them, some more valid than others. They are criticised for getting their election predictions wrong; for not really picking out what the electorate thinks; and for demeaning the political process by forcing politicians to prefer popular, irresponsible policies which improve their poll ratings to unpopular, responsible policies which damage them. It is worth examining these criticisms in turn.

'They get their predictions wrong'

In the US Presidential election of 1948 and the British general election of 1970 the polls predicted the wrong winner. (It is widely, but incorrectly, believed that they did so in February 1974 as well. In fact their prediction of the vote was extremely accurate; but the party which won most votes did not win most seats. The polls warned against rash interpretations of their findings but some newspapers ignored the warnings). But a poll cannot possibly predict a close election result infallibly. Every statistical prediction from a sample to a large population is of the form 'There is an x per cent chance (typically 95 or 99) that the population is not more than y per cent (typically two or three) away from the sample in its distribution of this attribute'. Close elections are often in the two-to-three per cent either-way range within which no practicable sampling procedure can be more precise, without an unmanageably large sample. (For more details see. e.g, McLean (1976) ch. 5, Teer and Spence (1975), Blalock (1960), chs. 9 to 11).

In any case, to concentrate on election result predictions is to miss the point of survey research. These predictions are the tip of the iceberg. They are melting, dirty, and not very interesting. Survey research matters not because it tells us how we would vote if there were a general election tomorrow (we all know in any case that there won't be) but because it asks more important questions that are not hypothetical. 'What do you think are the most important problems facing the country today?' 'Are you in favor of building more nuclear energy power plants, would you favor operating only those that are already built, or would you prefer to see all nuclear power plants closed down?' 'Some people think the Government should provide fewer services, even in areas such as health and education, in order to reduce spending. Other people feel it is important for the Government to continue the services it now provides even if it means no reduction in spending. Where would you place yourself on this scale?' (These are all questions used in reputable British or American surveys).

Nobody can (or should) doubt that these are real problems on which the electorate has real views. On some of them, people's views differ according to their class, region, colour, religion, sex, age, and so on; on some of them they do not. Modern statistical analysis can tell us very quickly if there is a 'significant' correlation between (say) class and attitudes to nuclear power. 'Significant' here has a technical meaning that is often abused or misunderstood. It means that a variation found in the sample is probably really there in the population from which the sample is drawn, and not just an accident arising from the chance of who happened to be in the sample. If we could have interviewed the whole population, we would probably have found a similar pattern. But 'significant' in the statistical sense doesn't necessarily mean significant in the everyday sense. And in any case a correlation is not an explanation. Conservative voters are systematically ('significantly') more likely than Labour voters to believe that 'the Queen and Royal Family are very important to Britain'.[6] This is a fact — not a particularly surprising one — but it does not explain itself. Do people become Conservative because they are monarchists, or monarchist because they are Conservatives, or both of these things because of some deeper underlying factor? Although such facts do not explain themselves, it is also true that they are facts which will not go away, and it is political Luddism to ignore them.

'Polls don't really tell us what the electorate thinks'

Many critics make this point. Some are Luddites; some are running away from uncomfortable facts; some have got a good point.

Politicians have always had ways of deciding for themselves what the voters are thinking. In late 1936, the Tory prime minister, Stanley Baldwin, watched Tory MPs' criticism of himself and support for Edward VIII in the Abdication crisis melt away over a weekend. He guessed that they had found out that there was no real public support for the king. 'I have always believed in the weekend', he said. 'But how they do it I don't know. I suppose they talk to the stationmaster'. Now that stationmasters have disappeared, their equivalents are probably taxi-drivers. The stationmaster (or taxi-driver) technique of sounding public opinion is certainly better than nothing; but it is silly to continue using it when better tools are at hand. In 1938 the editor of *The Times* told Neville Chamberlain that British public opinion favoured appeasing Hitler's Germany. At the same time, one of the first scientific opinion polls ever held in Britain showed that in Oxford readers of his own paper were more hostile to appeasement than any other group in the sample (see McLean 1973 and the sources cited there). Oxford may not have been typical; but any evidence, however patchy, is better than no evidence at all.

Many people still hold to the old ways, though. Norman Atkinson, a prominent left-wing MP on the National Executive of the Labour Party, recently dismissed opinion polls on the grounds that the management committee of his local Labour Party was a better yardstick of public opinion than the Gallup poll (cited in Butler and Kavanagh 1980, p. 272). But in fact the opinions of political activists differ, and differ systematically, from those of the general public. Politicians who ignore this important fact may lead themselves into serious trouble.

The valid part of this criticism was recently well expressed by the veteran commentator Henry Fairlie: 'In as complex an area as the motives of the electors, the polls in fact create their own answers by forming the questions'.[7] The biggest risk in interpreting survey evidence lies in assuming that the answers to every question carry a great deal of weight. Some do; some carry very little; some carry none at all. If a voter is asked what he thinks about some matter he has never or only vaguely heard of, he may feel he has to give an answer, out of politeness or to avoid sounding ignorant. Many questions which matter a great deal to politicians and administrators matter not at all to the average voter, and it would be a mistake to interpret voters' answers to them as if they did.

In a classic article, Converse (1964) showed how dangerous it is to build too grandly on shaky foundations. He analysed the answers to some attitude questions which the Survey Research Center at the University of Michigan put to the same sample three times at two-year intervals. On questions about, for instance, US federal aid to education or to overseas development, there were very low correlations between people's answers at the three sets of interviews. Although (say) 40 per cent of each sample might be for federal aid to education, it was a largely different 40 per cent each time.

This does not in itself prove that people give random or meaningless answers; they may have genuinely shifting views that just happen to cancel out. The original and disturbing part of

Converse's analysis was his closer examination of the answers to a question on whether private enterprise or government should be the main provider of housing and electricity. The three interviews threw up the pattern of correlations in Figure 1.1.

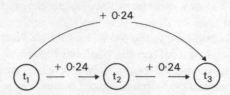

Figure 1.1 Stability of opinion over time: Michigan panel 1956-60

Source: Converse (1964) p. 242, substituting the tau-beta correlation value given at n.39 on p. 259 for that in the original

One would expect attitude changes either to be cumulative or to swing like a pendulum. If they were cumulative, the correlation between time 1 and time 3 would be much less than those over the two shorter periods. Some people would have changed their minds in the first interval, and some more in the second, with the result that the correlation between t_1 and t_3 would be the weakest. If the changes were pendulum-like, those who changed between t_1 and t_2 would change back between t_2 and t_3. Then the correlation between t_1 and t_3 would be stronger than the other two. For it to be the *same* is more puzzling, and, particularly if pendulum responses are disallowed as implausible, there is only one model that fits it. This model, not entirely plausible in itself yet neatly matching the contours of the data, divides the population rigorously into two groups: a group of 'stayers' who never change their minds, and a group of 'randomisers' who have no real opinion, and who choose an answer at random each time they are asked the question. The stayers have a correlation of 1 between any pair of their answers, and the randomisers a correlation of 0. Of course, an individual randomiser will sometimes, by chance, give the same answer twice or more often in a row. If the numbers on both sides of the question are the same, he has one chance in two of giving the same answer twice consecutively, and one in four of giving it three times consecutively.

Suppose we apply the model to Converse's observed correlations.

It stipulates that every subject who changed his answer was a randomiser. So were some who *didn't* change their answers — the model can tell us how many. Suppose, for simplicity, that the sample split fifty-fifty each time the question was asked. A randomiser then has a one-in-two chance of giving the same answer both times. We know how many changed their answers; we infer that the same number of people again were also randomisers even though they did not change their answers. So the subgroup who did not change from t_1 to t_2 contained a proportion of stayers with a predicted correlation of 1 to t_3 and a proportion of randomisers with a predicted correlation of 0. Combining these two in the correct proportion produced a predicted correlation of 0.47 for those who did not change in the first interval. The prediction for those who did change was, of course, 0. The actual correlations in the sample were 0.49 and 0.004 respectively (Converse 1964, p. 259).

This is an important finding, and readers should try to grasp its implications even if they are a little baffled by the last two paragraphs. Converse proved that public 'opinion' on one topic moved in a way which can be plausibly explained only by assuming that some people had no real opinion at all, and gave random answers each time they were asked the question. If this conclusion were generally applicable, there would be no point in writing this book. I believe that it is not generally applicable, but that it does — or at least may — apply to a very large range of questions on which politicians have views but many voters have not. I have tried not to draw any conclusions about voters' opinions on issues which are not *salient* to them. In a recent poll, 27 per cent of an American sample favoured the ratification of the SALT II nuclear arms restriction treaty with the Soviet Union. Nine per cent opposed it. But 64 per cent offered no opinion.[8] The Don't Knows had it, and it would be wrong to analyse the opinions of the Do Knows and present them as those of the electorate. Many, even of those who did present an opinion, certainly had no real one.

There are some practical ways of telling which issues matter to electors. One is very simple: ask them. Questions like 'What do you think are the most important problems facing the country today?' produce a pretty consistent series of answers in surveys. Economic problems almost always dominate all others in voters' minds. Inflation or unemployment or strikes or more than one of these is invariably in the top three. Problems of public order and social welfare tend to come next. Many of the key concerns of governments, and above all foreign policy, usually come much lower in the electorate's list. When foreign affairs do become salient, it is usually because 'our boys' are, or might be, involved. The British electorate did not worry much about Hitler until the Munich crisis of September 1938, when it suddenly looked as if there might be a war with Germany over Czechoslovakia. Chamberlain's cri-de-coeur, 'How horrible, fantastic, incredible it is that we should be digging trenches and trying on gas-masks here because of a quarrel in a faraway country between people of whom we know nothing' was widely condemned as a highly irresponsible thing for a statesman to say. Maybe it was. But it was much closer to the mood of the people than were Winston Churchill's warnings (McLean 1973). Now that Britain is no longer a world power, the British people know even less about faraway countries than they did in 1938. Likewise, Vietnam became 'a problem' in the eye of most Americans only when their sons and brothers started being killed there and the war reached the corner of everybody's living-room. Iran became 'a problem' in 1979−80 because 52 American hostages were locked up there. Far fewer Americans saw the simultaneous Soviet invasion of Afghanistan as a serious problem.

None of this is meant to be condescending to the electorate, and it is foolishly elitist to use this evidence to poke fun at the ignorance of voters. Politicians are politicians all or most of the time. Electors are politicians for only a very small part of the time, and it is quite unfair to expect ordinary voters to spend their time acquiring political knowledge which they will never use. Nonetheless, we must not forget that electors have no real views on many issues of public policy. If we do forget, we may be building elaborate turreted castles on sand.

Another quick test of the importance to voters of an issue is to check the proportion who say they 'don't know' when asked their view in a survey. A recent US national survey gives some typical results. 'Do you think your income has kept up with inflation?' (concrete question, salient subject) generated only 1.8 per cent of don't knows. The question about nuclear power stations quoted at p. 13 above (concrete question, non-salient subject) generated 7.7 per cent. With more abstract and/or hypothetical questions, the number of don't knows shoots up, 34.8 per cent of the sample would not place themselves on a seven-point scale from 'extremely liberal' to 'extremely conservative' and 47.6 per cent of it were unwilling to place Ronald Reagan on the same scale. (A further 1.2 per cent thought he was 'extremely liberal'.)[9] These statistics convey an unmistakable warning.

'Polls demean the political process'

The third main criticism of opinion polls takes us deep into the realm of value judgments. Widespread knowledge of the findings of attitude surveys, according to the critics, makes candidates bow to every fickle whim of a chance electoral majority. This makes responsible policy-making impossible. Moreover, the polls make politicians more likely to listen to special interest groups with an axe to grind. A minority which feels intensely on one side of a subject is more likely to voice its opinions than a majority which feels less intensely on the other.

There is something in both of these points. Politicians often do behave like that. For example, surveys document the continuing refusal of the American people to believe that the USA faces a real shortage of oil; people commonly attribute the shortages and price rises they see around them to greed and hoarding by the oil companies. It does not take much to know that this view is false; yet Ronald Reagan, as Republican presidential candidate in 1980, claimed that there was indeed no real energy shortage in the USA. At the same time, both major candidates were falling over each other in their eagerness to make offers to identifiable minorities. Within weeks of Jimmy Carter's campaign medal for an Italian-American who had never got one for his Second World War service, Ronald Reagan was telling Hispanic-Americans in southern Texas that he would introduce an amnesty for illegal immigrants from Mexico to the USA.

But that is not the polls' fault. To blame them is to blame the messenger for the message. Politicians chased special-interest groups long before there were polls to show them the way. If opinion polls did not exist, politicians would use other means of finding out what the electorate thought. They are under pressure from lobbying groups which would be just as heavy if polls did not exist. Polls do indeed provide some independent check on whether a lobby has as much support as it claims. If it is bad to do what a fickle majority wants, it is presumably worse to do what you incorrectly think a fickle majority wants. Asking stationmasters, or constituency management committees, what the people want is more perilous than finding out from the Gallup Poll.

This dispute opens up a deep problem of democracy. There are many issues where a politician may know that most of the voters are just plain wrong — as in the American energy case. There are more which are matters not of right or wrong, but of conflicting values, and many politicians will wish to maintain their views even in the face of evidence that the electorate is against them. A typical list might include protection of civil rights, opposition to capital punishment, and refusal to subsidise loss-making industries. Most democratic politicians have other values which sometimes conflict with democracy; they sometimes put democracy first, and sometimes the conflicting value or values. No commentator can tell them which is the 'right' thing to do; there is no right and wrong in the making of value-based decisions. That is inescapably part of a politician's task. The argument that polls push him towards a 'wrong' decision is doubly flawed. Not only would the pressure be there whether the polls existed or not, but the concept of a 'right' or 'wrong' decision is baseless.

THE DEDUCTIVE APPROACH

There is a third, quite different, way of looking at voting behaviour. The geographical and survey approaches examine what voters actually do (or think); the deductive approach examines what they would do if they were individuals rationally pursuing their goals in a highly simplified model world. It then gradually makes its model world more complicated in order to make it resemble the real world more closely. Finally, it compares its findings with what actually happens in the real world, in the hope that the model-building process will throw some light on why and how real people do the things they do.

The best way to get the flavour of this sort of argument is to follow a deductive line of reasoning through. Chapter 4 will do this in some detail; as a sampler, I shall present here the best-known argument in Downs (1957), the most important pioneer work in this field.

Suppose I live in a street of identically spaced houses all on the same side — nos. 1 to 100. I do all my shopping in the street and will always buy my goods from the nearest shop. At which number should a shopkeeper set up his business if he believes one rival may come into the street? The answer is exactly half-way along at no. 50. Then any rival can, at best, set up shop next door — say at no. 51. In that event, the first trader has all the business from nos. 1 to 50 inclusive and the second has all the business from 51 to 100 inclusive: an even split. But suppose either the first or the second trader sets up somewhere away from the middle. If the first goes to no. 20, the second has only to go to no. 21 to gain four-fifths of the trade. If one shop is already established at no. 50, a rival which sets up at no. 70 will do less well because only 61 to 100 will do business with him; everybody else will shop at no. 50.

The next step is to turn the housekeepers into voters and the shopkeepers into political parties. The model now implies that if voters are evenly spread out along some ideological spectrum, a party which wants to win an election should offer what the median voter wants — that is, the voter with exactly as many people on one side of him as on the other. The best that another party can do is to come as close as possible. So the parties will converge, offering almost identical bundles of policies to the electorate: policies which they both believe the median elector will support.

The third step is to complicate the model to take account of some of the objections which most readers will already be making. We shall do this in Chapter 4. Here are some of the questions, though the answers (where there are any) will have to wait. What if voters are not evenly spread out along the ideological street? If the parties tend to converge, won't extremist voters stay at home rather than bother to vote? If the parties become *exactly* identical, why should anybody bother to vote at all? What happens if it is easy to form new parties? What will citizens who want to move the parties away from convergence do?

Finally, we carry the model across to the real world, and put it down beside the real world to see whether it shows us any recognizable features of actual voters and actual parties. Even in its simplest form, it does. Major parties in Britain and America, and in most other democracies, proclaim widely differing philosophies, but often offer surprisingly similar policies in election campaigns (and even more often behave similarly in government). Every so often, party activists rebel against the 'consensus' or 'middle ground', and demand that the party should offer 'a choice, not an echo', in the memorable words of Barry Goldwater, the US Republican Presidential candidate in 1964. But Goldwater's own fate is instructive. The voters saw the choice and voted for the echo; Lyndon Johnson (D) was elected by a landslide majority. Eight years later, the Democrats nominated George McGovern, a candidate with strong appeals to the disaffected young, the poor, and the black. Having ignored Scammon and Wattenberg's (1970) timely warning that most Americans were unyoung, unpoor and unblack, the Democrats crashed to a defeat as crushing as Goldwater's. (For more detail, see Page 1978; Nie, Verba and Petrocik 1979 ch. 18).

In Britain, both Margaret Thatcher and Tony Benn are proudly conscious of pulling their parties away from consensus. Some academics (notably Finer 1975 and 1980) agree on the description, but disagree on their appraisal. They regard 'adversary politics' as evidence that the British party system is distorted and unresponsive to what the people actually want. Both the politicians and the academics are criticised by Rose (1980a), who argues that the evidence that adversary politics actually exists in Britain is patchy. Whatever people said in opposition (itself not always adversary), they usually did the same things in government, according to Rose; and on some things, such as disliking proportional representation, the supposed adversaries are warm allies. Though the last remains true, reality since 1979 has undoubtedly moved away from Rose and towards Finer.

In any case, the position of the British parties in 1980-81 in no way makes the Downsian model look unrealistic. It is true that the Conservative Government is remote from the median voter. But so is the Labour opposition, especially the National Executive Committee and the leadership of the Labour Party outside Parliament. The shopkeepers are at nos. 25 and 75, and doing adequate business — not much less than if they were at 50 and 51, and much more popular with the people at no. 1 and no. 100, who have not so far to walk to their nearest shop as they used to. But on 24 March 1981, the Social Democratic Party announced that it was going to occupy the empty Co-op at no. 50. (For details, see Bradley 1981). If the Labour and Conservative Parties move back to nos. 49 and 51 for the next General Election, they will leave the new party short of custom; if at least one of them does not, it may do

TABLE 3.3

USA: POPULATION BY RACE AND COUNTRY OF BIRTH 1880–1970

Year	White native born Number (000s)	%	White foreign born n	%	Negro n	%	Other n	%
1880	43,403	76.5	6,560	11.6	6,581	11.6	172	0.3
1920	94,821	79.4	13,712	11.5	10,463	8.8	466	0.4
1970	177,749	83.8	8,734	4.1	22,580	10.7	2883	1.4

Source: US Bureau of the Census (1975). Derived from Tables A 119-34.

they inhabited were bargained or bought into the USA. Today, they guard their separate identity more fiercely than most ethnic groups, with an elaborate network of Spanish-language institutions, including radio and TV channels in every city in the South-western states. Strategists of both parties have identified them as a key group of floating voters, and wooed them assiduously; but many of them stay aloof from American politics. Their main importance is their contribution to making the USA a land of non-voters — it has the lowest electoral turnouts of any democracy, and has had habitually since the 1890s.

Like their contemporaries, the Founding Fathers did not think of Indians as real people with real rights. The Constitution, with its casual references to 'excluding Indians not taxed', and to Congress's power to 'regulate Commerce with foreign Nations, and among the several States, and with the Indian Tribes', makes this plain. When they became citizens, their numbers were so decimated by war and disease that they were electorally insignificant, though they probably give a plurality of their votes to the Democrats.

Very few of the nineteenth-century European immigrants to the USA arrived with any party affiliations, as they did not come from democratic countries. When they did have affiliations, these were usually organised around quite different cleavages to those discussed so far. The immigrants became assimilated to American politics essentially because their leaders realised that political machinery could be used to deliver welfare to the ethnic community. There were no Social Security checks or employment exchanges for them. But if the 'machine' controlled the city, it could arrange for benefits for people in distress, or jobs on the city's payroll. The other side of the bargain was votes: votes which ensured that the 'machine' or the 'organisation' continued to control the city.

The city machine has not had a good press. The Progressives thought it was corrupt and undemocratic, and tried to kill it off. More recently, some more sympathetic commentators have stressed that the machine did smooth off some rough edges for poor foreign immigrants, and that offering jobs in return for votes need not be considered any more corrupt than offering goods in return for money. If being a grocer is not inherently corrupt, perhaps being a machine politician is not either.

We shall return to this in Chapters 6 and 8. For now, the important point is the impact of the machines on party politics. The earliest ones were Irish, and they were Democratic, probably because from the outset the Democrats represented 'democratic' and not 'aristocratic passions'. But not all machines have been Democratic. When a new wave of immigrants arrived in a city to find the last group already entrenched, there was a direct clash of interests, since only one ethnic group could control welfare and patronage at a time. Thus some machines (such as the Italians' in New York City) have been Republican, not Democratic.

Their influence should not be overstated. Many immigrants lay outside it, and they were socialised more slowly and in a different way. There is some evidence (Nie *et al.* 1979 ch. 5; Andersen 1979) that the New Deal realignment of 1928-36 arose partly because immigrants and the children of immigrants voted for the first time in these elections, where previously they were not naturalised, or if naturalised were not politicised. We must now turn to the three great realignments, in order to relate the cleavages that we have discussed so far to the changing fortunes and social bases of the parties.

THE PARTY SYSTEM AND THE GREAT REALIGNMENTS

Since Key's (1955) seminal article on the election of 1928 there has been intense academic interest in 'critical' or 'realigning' elections: those which mark a permanent change in the voting habits of some large group(s) in the electorate. Much of the debate has been unnecessarily confused. For instance, people are already hailing 1980 as a realigning election; but, by definition, a single election cannot demonstrate whether voting changes are permanent or not. Also, some of the disputants have talked past one another as one side points to changes in votes and the other to changes in party identification. Since these are not the same thing, both sides could be right. I shall therefore not go into the debate in detail. (Readers who wish to do so can find useful summaries and pointers in Niemi and Weisberg 1976 chs 1, 24, and 27). Everybody agrees, however, that there were fundamental shifts in Presidential voting behaviour in 1856-61, 1892-6 and 1928-36. These are the three great realignments of the era of mass franchise.

The realignment of 1856 came because the cleavages of region and race came to overshadow that of class. Neither existing party —

the Whigs and the Democrats — could cope with the slavery issue as two crises became more pressing: where would slavery be permitted as settlement moved westwards? and could slaves who escaped into a non-slave state be freed, or was that an illegal incursion into their owners' property rights? Both parties split at least three ways. Those at one extreme wanted slavery to be abolished even in the South; those at the other wanted no legal restrictions at all on its spread; the rest lay uncomfortably in between at various compromise positions. By 1856 the Whig party had disintegrated altogether. The Democrats were more cohesive, but they split in 1860. The Republican party was formed in 1856 as a coalition between outright abolitionists and those who were prepared to see slavery continued in the South but not elsewhere (Lincoln was in the second camp. He was not an abolitionist. For him, the great principle was saving the Union, not abolishing slavery). The Republicans fought unsuccessfully in 1856, and won in 1860. The Democrats still had a plurality of the popular vote in that year, but they were crippled by their split and by the geographical distribution of the vote. Each wing of the party remained strong in its part of the country. But the South has too few electoral votes to carry the country, and in the North the Democrats ran narrowly but consistently behind the Republicans, who thus got an absolute majority of the electoral vote with under 40 per cent of the popular vote and no support at all in a large part of the country. As we have seen, these events drove the whole South into the arms of the Democratic party.

In the realignment of 1892-6, region again crosscut class, with religion playing a subsidiary role. Struggling Mid-western and Southern farmers first of all formed the Populist party to express their grievances against their creditors, and then captured the Democratic party with the nomination of William Jennings Bryan of Nebraska to be the party's presidential candidate in 1896. Bryan's call for free silver — 'you shall not crucify mankind on a cross of gold' — also attracted the Mountain West states which had recently joined the Union. But Bryan neither understood nor cared about the problems of urban labour and the cities, which were acute because of depression and harsh employers' attacks on trade unions. 'Burn down your cities and leave our farms, and your cities will spring up again as if by magic; but destroy our farms and the grass will grow in the streets of every city in the country'.[6] Bryan's use of 'your' and 'our' is almost as expressive as the sentiment itself. He was also a Protestant fundamentalist and prohibitionist, neither of them causes with much resonance in the urban North-east.

The 1896 result was not actually a Republican landslide (the popular vote was 7 million Republican and 6.5 million Democratic), though writers often speak as if it were. But it did usher in a spell of Republican ascendancy that lasted until the next realignment, that of 1928-36. In 1928 the Democrats for the first time adopted a candidate who really appealed to city voters. Alfred E. Smith was an Irish Catholic New Yorker who opposed Prohibition. Key's (1955) ecological analysis shows that it was in 1928 that the Democratic vote turned around sharply in urban Catholic precincts in New England.

The New Deal coalition was three elections and eight years in the forming. In 1932 F. D. Roosevelt's campaign platform was as conservative as Herbert Hoover's, but enough people turned out to vote for him out of dissatisfaction with Hoover's failure to deal with unemployment or the collapse of farm prices to give the Democrats over 50 per cent of the vote for the first time since 1876.[7] But the full coalition of labour, blacks, 'ethnics' and the white South, with a gilding of Eastern college professors, did not come into existence until the Democratic landslide of 1936. Andersen's ecological data for Chicago (Table 3.4) neatly illustrate the steps which built the coalition.

TABLE 3.4

DEMOCRATIC SHARE OF THE TWO-PARTY PRESIDENTIAL VOTE 1924–40: SELECTED WARDS IN CHICAGO

Year	Immigrant wards %	White Native Wards %	Black Wards %
1924	38	17	8
1928	60	26	30
1932	71	48	24
1936	81	53	48
1940	76	42	48

Source: Andersen (1979), Table 15, p. 100

The big jump came in 1928 in immigrant areas, in 1932 in native-stock areas and in 1936 in black areas. As ever we must beware of the ecological fallacy, but these data cry out for one interpretation: that the dominant group in the ward in question switched to, or turned out for the first time to vote for, the Democrats in the year of the big jump.

All three alignments, indeed, owe at least as much to turnout changes and turnover in the electorate as to voters who changed sides. The 1856-60 and 1928-36 realignments featured increases in turnout and the middle one a drop. So mobilisation or demobilisation of voters probably played a bigger role in the realignments than conversion. The Republican party was broader-based than its Whig predecessor, a fact which probably pushed up the turnout in 1856 and 1860. Then the retreat of the Democrats to the countryside left many city-dwellers in 1896 more than ever without a party worth making the effort to vote for. Finally, the New Deal realignment drew many people into voting for the first time, particularly among those who had entered the USA in the last big wave of immigration (1900-20) and their children. The average time between arrival and naturalisation was eleven years (Andersen 1979 p. 88), and many of the immigrants were not politicised into the American party system until some years after their naturalisation.

Since journalists discovered the concept of critical elections there has been intense speculation as to whether there has been another realignment or not. Every presidential election since 1964 has been hailed as 'the' realigning one, except 1976, which was hailed as the reinstating one in which the old Democratic coalition had been rebuilt. Some people, indeed, have a mystical belief that a realignment must happen every thirty years (the two previous accepted cases are 1800 and 1828). However, a realignment must show a pattern which persists over at least two elections, and no pair of presidential elections since 1964 has done. There has been a substantial *de*alignment. The New Deal coalition has collapsed; 1976 was not a reinstating election, as 1980 has shown, and the white South seems to have disappeared for ever from the presidential and (especially) congressional Democratic lists. In 1980, the Democrats lost Senate races in Alabama and Georgia for the first time since Reconstruction and had a close call in Arkansas.

The evidence for dealignment is not only in the fluctuating

fortunes of the parties. The decline in turnout and party identification and the rise of issue voting also point that way. 1980 was a triumph for issue voting, not for the Republican Party. So we must look at the evidence for the rise of issue voting.

THE ISSUES AND THE RISE OF ISSUE VOTING

Since the late 1940s Gallup and other survey organisations have frequently asked random samples of Americans what they think are the most important problems facing the American people. The answers show elements of both stability and change, and the data for the survey nearest to each presidential election since 1956 are given in Table 3.5.

How does this pattern differ from the British one? Primarily in that foreign affairs seem to count for much more. In every election year except 1976 a foreign issue was at least the second most popular candidate for the American people's most important problem. An obvious reason for the difference is that the USA is a world power and Britain is not. So the USA is far more deeply embroiled in world crises, most acutely in ones in which Americans are killed in foreign countries: Korea from 1949 to 1952, Vietnam from 1963 to 1972, Iran in 1980.

The full series of surveys from which Table 3.5 has been extracted implies that foreign policy problems come in two classes. Either they are both acute and salient, or they are neither. The Vietnam and Iran crises are in the first category. In January 1980, as Table 3.5 shows, *CBS News* found 42 per cent of Americans to be most worried about foreign affairs (mostly Iran). In June 1979 the same survey had found only three per cent naming a foreign issue and 31 per cent naming energy. At that time the Iranian revolution threatened America's gasoline supply but not her diplomats. Foreign policy crises become important to most Americans when and only when American lives are at stake. American 'advisors' started going to Vietnam in 1963, and by late 1964 the USA was already being sucked in deeper and deeper. Vietnam was an issue on which the candidates in 1964 took sharply opposed views, but it was not yet a salient one for the public because American deaths had not begun.

The explanation for the salience of foreign policy in the 1950s must be different. People were not passionately concerned about

TABLE 3.5

'THE MOST IMPORTANT PROBLEM FACING THE AMERICAN PEOPLE TODAY':
THREE MOST POPULAR ANSWERS, PRESIDENTIAL ELECTION YEARS 1956–80

Issue area	Month and Year												
	10/56		9/59		9/64		6/68		9/72		11/76 to 1/77		1/80	
	%	Rank	%	Rank	%	Rank	%	Rank	%	Rank	%	Rank	%	Rank
War, foreign affairs (except Vietnam)	48	1	51	1	16	2							42	1
Econ. problems (eg unemp., inflation)	23	2	21	2	10	3			30	1	63	1	37	2
Civil rights, integration	12	3	5	3	35	1	13	3						
Vietnam							52	1	27	2				
Crime, drugs							29	2	19	3	5	3		
Energy											5	2	10	3

Sources: 1956 to 1972, Gallup Poll. Cited in Nie et al (1979) Table 6.1, pp. 100-103. September 1959 is nearest month given to 1960 election.
1976, CPS post-election survey, University of Michigan. Percentages calculated from frequencies given in Inter-University Consortium for Political and Social Research (1977), Vol. 2, pp. 772-3.
1980, CBS News nationwide poll. Cited in *Public Opinion*, February/March 1980, p. 21.

the spread of world communism; they were just unconcerned about anything much else. Joseph McCarthy and others had largely created the issue of Communism by whipping up hysteria about it, but otherwise the period was one of exceptional political blandness — a phrase used over and over again by Nie *et al.* (1979) in criticising their predecessors Campbell *et al.* (1960) for making assumptions for all time about voters' ignorance and low issue concern which turn out to have been true only for the 1950s. Then, in both Britain and the USA, people felt they had 'never had it so good'. They were much poorer than they are now, of course; but compared to what they had expected they were satisfied. Now that people expect more and get less, economic issues seem to be as dominant in the USA as in Britain, as the 1976 data eloquently show, except when an Iran crisis comes along to push them out of people's minds.

How do these issues relate to the parties, politicians and cleavages discussed so far? Abroad, citizens want America to be a world power, but do not want Americans to die overseas for causes they do not understand. It is not always easy to reconcile these objectives. Citizens, and politicians too, shift their priorities from one to the other in ways that are not always logical or easy to chart. There is a vague feeling, which Republicans trade on when it is convenient, that they are the 'peace party' and the Democrats are the 'war party'. Democratic administrations took the US into both world wars, Korea and Vietnam; Republican ones got America out of the last two and dominated the long isolationist period. At the same time Republicans, especially freelance right-wingers, also castigate Democrats for 'weakness' such as that of Truman which supposedly led to the 'loss of China' in 1949 and the inability of the Carter administration to rescue the American hostages in Iran.

Foreign policy may seem to comprise 'position' rather than 'valence' issues. All the crises mentioned in the last paragraph presented politicians with stark choices, and one might expect voters to line up clearly on one side or the other. But they do not. Most of the aims of most Americans are 'valence' ones: both for their country to be a super-power and for its citizens not to be killed abroad, for instance. Electors have to choose between these objectives far less often than politicians do. However, politicians are rewarded or punished for what they do overseas. Lyndon Johnson was punished in 1968 for getting America into Vietnam and Richard Nixon was rewarded in 1972 for getting America out. But, especially early in the campaigns, voters did not express clear-cut ideologies. In 1968, Johnson decided not to run again after an anti-war candidate, Eugene McCarthy, had done well in the early Democratic primaries. But surveys (Niemi and Weisberg 1976, pp. 210-1) show that McCarthy's early support came as much from people who thought that Johnson had done too little in Vietnam as from those who thought he had done too much. At that stage, the valence view that something was wrong in Vietnam, and that it was Lyndon Johnson's fault, predominated. Later in the campaign, as the issues were more discussed, this view faded in favour of position views on one side or the other.

Economic affairs are likewise more valence than position. Most voters dislike both unemployment and inflation, and politicians of all shades of opinion take their cue from this. As with foreign policy, there is a trade-off. Attempts to lower one of these evils may raise the other. But for the most part politicians stress the valence aspect. Their attitude to both unemployment and inflation is that they are against them.

Energy almost became a position issue in the 1970s. By 1980, the independent presidential candidate John Anderson set himself sharply against the major candidates with a call for a stiff gasoline tax to cut fuel consumption. (Even his 50 cents a gallon could not have raised prices to even two-thirds of European levels; but it would have been a 40 per cent increase.) The impact of the issue was muffled by citizens' widespread ignorance of the real energy position of the USA and the world, but it could be an important position issue in years to come.

Crime, drugs and integration are the other three issues that have made the top three since 1956. Crime is a pure valence issue; integration and civil rights a pure position issue; drugs somewhere in between. All three featured in voters' responses to the insurgent presidential candidates George Wallace (breakaway Democrat, 1968) and George McGovern (Democrat, 1972). Wallace built up a coalition of white southerners angered by civil rights and 'hard-hat' blue-collar Northern city-dwellers upset by the rise of crime, violence and drug-taking in the cities. His unexpected success (with 13.5 per cent of the popular vote and 46 electoral votes in the Deep South) prompted Scammon and Wattenberg (1970) to give two warnings: that the 'Social Issue', uniting concern about crime, drugs and violent demonstrations, was rising to prominence, and that any candidate who took the side of the young, the poor, or the black — voters likely to be on the minority side on at least one component of the 'Social Issue' — must remember that most Americans were unyoung and unpoor and unblack. McGovern, or more precisely his most active backers, forgot this lesson, so that he fell to the worst presidential defeat of a Democrat since 1924. However, the 'Social Issue' had faded a little. Table 3.5 shows that its components no longer get into the top three. This is partly because most (not quite all) voters now accept the fait accompli of civil rights; partly because that legislation itself guaranteed Southern blacks' position in the electorate; partly because politicians have stopped trying to push action on behalf of minorities beyond the limits which Wallacites would tolerate without rebelling again. In November 1980, for instance, the US Senate finally bowed to the massive white opposition to 'busing' of school children in order to achieve a racial mix in public schools, and voted to abandon federal support for the practice.

It is impossible to study recent American politics, and especially the campaigns of McGovern, Wallace, and Barry Goldwater in 1964, without noticing the difference from the Eisenhower years during which Campbell *et al.* (1960) did their pioneering work. Then there were few issues and fewer position issues. Eisenhower was elected in 1952 and 1956 because he was a war hero, not because he took any particular issue positions. It is not surprising that the Michigan investigators found a low level of knowledge and concern about politics among their samples. The position has changed substantially. Just as the instant commentators have discovered the Michigan consensus about the ignorance of the electorate, the academics have finally abandoned it (Niemi and Weisberg 1976, pp. 66-159; Nie *et al.* 1979, *passim* esp. chs. 7-10). Some of the original work, notably Converse's seminal article (1964; see ch. 1 above) remains valid; but some now looks like an overgeneralisation from an unusually bland period. The mean level of American voters' education has risen substantially since 1956, but the rise of issue voting is more than a mere consequence of that. Levels of issue voting and 'consistency' (a tricky concept which I examine below) have risen among people at all educational levels, and those with minimal education are now, on average, more ideological than those with college degrees were in 1956 (Nie *et al.* 1979, pp. 120, 149.)

The rise of issue is linked to the decline of party. In every democracy except the USA, parties are handy brand labels. If a voter buys a pack of Labour education policy and likes it because of its working-class flavour, he has grounds to expect that Labour housing policy, which he has not yet tasted, also has that agreeable working-class flavour. But this does not happen in the USA, for familiar historical reasons. In each presidential election from 1964 to 1972 at least one candidate was offering a distinctive bundle of policies whose contents could not be predicted from his party label; and in 1980 John B. Anderson abandoned labelling altogether. His own-brand, partyless (but not issueless) product achieved six per cent of the market. Meanwhile the decline in party identification has continued; and, at least in congressional races, voters seem to have responded to issues raised by single-issue pressure groups.

In addition, there is a deep flaw in the method used by even the revisionist scholars who found that 'issue consistency' had been rising. But for the flaw, they might have found that the voters were even more issue-oriented. A typical method is to pack attitudes into 'left-wing' and 'right-wing' bundles, or 'liberal', 'moderate' and 'conservative' ones. These are similar to the packages which mainstream politicians offer the voters. For example, many politicians who called themselves liberal in the 1960s favoured civil rights for black Americans, heavy government intervention in the economy, high welfare spending and a relatively soft approach to the Soviet Union. Most politicians who called themselves conservative took the opposite side on all four. The Michigan analysts and their followers showed that correlations between voters' attitudes to the items in these bundles were low. If a voter took a 'liberal' view on one, there were no grounds for predicting that he would take a 'liberal' view on the next. Voters' 'issue consistency' was low, although it rose in the late 1960s to the early 1970s.

But this procedure is arrogant and unacceptable. It shows that voters do not pack their preferences up into the same bundles as politicians do. But who has the right to say that voters are being inconsistent? Converse pointed out (1964, pp. 211-13), in a message most of his followers failed to heed, that the constraints which bind preferences together into 'liberal' and 'conservative' bundles are not usually logical ones. There is no logical reason in the world why I should not simultaneously oppose black civil rights and favour détente with the Soviet Union. The constraints are largely accidental:

that is the way party systems happen to have grown up. Voters have ideologies which correspond roughly, but only roughly, with politicians'. This was shown by Stimson (1976), who applied a statistical technique called factor analysis to 1972 Michigan data. Factor analysis does not assume in advance that associations between attitudes 'ought' to follow a particular pattern; it merely looks for patterns that happen to be there, leaving the problem of interpreting them to the investigator. It is important to realise that the number of possible patterns multiplies very quickly with the number of issues. Stimson used eleven attitude questions. If the number of possible positions on each question is reduced from the original seven to three (for, against, or indifferent), there are still 3^{11} $= 177,147$ possible 'ideologies'. That is about a hundred times as many ideologies as there were people in the sample. If only two people had had the same ideology that would already be some evidence of consistency. It is much more appropriate to be surprised that consistency is as high as it is than surprised that it is as low as it is.

If the voters are out of line with the politicians, deductive theories such as those we examine in the next chapter imply that the politicians will probably fall into line and change their attitudes. American evidence suggests that this is happening. George Wallace crosscut party lines in 1968 in order to articulate an ideology that was shared by many voters. Sometimes voters change their minds about issues. In the past, people of generally liberal and egalitarian views favoured extensive government intervention on behalf of disadvantaged groups. Many of them no longer do, and politicians have started to say the same things.[8] Does this make them inconsistent? No, the issues have changed, and both voters and politicians have changed with them. There is nothing inconsistent in that.

4

The rational-choice approach

> And we define: the democratic method is that institutional arrangement for arriving at political decisions in which individuals acquire the power to decide by means of a competitive struggle for the people's vote.
>
> J. A. Schumpeter, 1942

RATIONALITY IN CLASSICAL POLITICAL THOUGHT

The deductive approach has a long history. The greatest pioneer was Thomas Hobbes (1588-1679), whose *Leviathan* was published in 1651. Hobbes thought that 'Geometry is the onely Science that it hath pleased God hitherto to bestow on mankind', and hoped to set up a whole deductive science of society from what he thought were elementary axioms and definitions of rational behaviour. Hobbes thought that rational man would see that life in the state of nature must be 'solitary, poore, nasty, brutish, and short', and that the only way to escape was to agree to set up Leviathan, a ruler with absolute authority.

Hobbes's model was not based on observation, any more than geometry is based on observation. You do not prove Pythagoras's Theorem by drawing lots of right-angled triangles, measuring their sides, and finding out that the square of the length of the hypotenuse always equals the sum of the squares of the length of the other two sides. You prove it by starting from elementary definitions and axioms ('the shortest distance between two points is a straight line') and gradually making more and more elaborate deductions, ending with something perhaps unexpected ('By God, this is impossible!', said Hobbes when he first read Pythagoras's Theorem) but inescapably true if the starting definitions are acceptable and the axioms valid.

But there is a crucial difference between geometry and human behaviour, a difference which Hobbes did not fully appreciate. Abstract mathematical statements are in no way statements about real things or people. Mathematics (including geometry) is a closed system making tautological statements. But an axiom of human rationality does at least sound like a statement about the real world. Look again at Downs's definition of a rational man (quoted on p. 23 above). The whole impressive structure he builds rests on this foundation. If the foundation cracks — if men in the real world are *not* like that — it seems that the whole house will tumble down.

Many analysts after Hobbes assumed with little question that some axioms of human rationality were valid. Men knew what they wanted in politics, and in democratic politics they would vote for the politician or party offering policies nearest to those they preferred. To do this, they had to know where the parties stood on the issues of the day. These assumptions underlie, for instance, Mill (1972; first published 1861) and were taken up by countless lesser writers.

They were undermined by hard evidence that the world was not like that. Psychologists stressed the irrationality of some mass behaviour, or at least redefined rationality in a way which was incompatible with Hobbes's (or Downs's) axioms. People participate in politics to get various forms of psychic gratification — the warmth of being one of a crowd, the love and respect of one's followers (See e.g. Wallas 1948 — originally published in 1908). The rise of hysterical, irrational, anti-democratic mass movements with — paradoxically — widespread popular support underlined the point. Hitler and Mussolini seemed far removed from the world of J. S. Mill.

The first survey researchers nevertheless clung to the belief that voters chose among parties and policies as they might choose among apples and oranges at a wayside stall. When they found out that voters were not like that, they wondered with dismay whether their findings undermined the whole of democratic theory (Berelson *et al.* 1954, ch. 14). This line culminated in the Michigan surveys of the 1950s and in Converse's (1964) article discussed in Chapter 1.

Nevertheless, the deductive method has had a great revival, and has now become once again a leading mode of inquiry into all sorts of political science and political theory. The two leading works of modern political philosophy — Rawls (1972) and Nozick (1974) — go back explicitly to a Hobbesian state of nature and use Hobbes's tools of analysis, though for some reason both are curiously reluctant to acknowledge their intellectual debts to Hobbes. In the field of voters' and politicians' behaviour many scholars are following the road first surveyed by Schumpeter (1954, chs. 20 to 23; first published in 1942) and then hacked out by Downs (1957). The deductive analyst has two defences against the criticisms of psychologists and the Michigan school. First, evidence that voters do not think of issues in 'left-wing' or 'right-wing' ways, nor know what many of the issues, as defined by the politicians, even are, is no evidence that the voters are irrational. No reasonable definition of rationality should require people to sort their political attitudes into some preordained pattern, or to trouble to find out about things which concern them very little. Secondly, modern rational-choice theorists avoid the mistake of saying that they can deduce how society *is* or *must be.* They can analyse how society *would be* if their starting axiom of rationality were valid. They can generate 'testable propositions derived from the theory' (the title of the final chapter of Downs 1957). The next step is to test some: such as 'Democratic governments tend to favor producers more than consumers in their actions' (Downs 1957, p. 297). We shall look at this particular one in Chapter 5. If we find it is true, the rational choice model helps explain a non-obvious fact. If we find it is false, that does not necessarily condemn the model. Its reasoning may still be valid but its axioms false. If people *were* rational in the way it stipulates, the consequence would be X. X is not the case. Therefore we can conclude that people are not rational in the way defined at the outset. That is in itself an important finding.

It is time now to look at the two main decisions which the theory examines: the decision whether or not to vote at all, and the decision what party to vote for.

WHY VOTE AT ALL?

Voting sometimes produces benefits and always involves costs. The main benefit occurs if and only if a citizen's vote helps to install a government he approves of, though he may get subsidiary benefits such as helping to save democracy from the collapse that would occur if nobody voted, and meeting his friends at the poll, or on the way there or back. There are costs in shoeleather, bus fares or petrol, and an 'opportunity cost' in that the time he spends voting cannot simultaneously be spent on something pleasurable or productive such as weeding the garden or having sex with his girlfriend. In a Downsian world, the rational citizen will vote if the benefits outweigh the costs and abstain if they do not. So which are usually greater, the benefits or the costs?

This may seem to be a stupid question. Surely a fervent Labour supporter will rank the chance to save himself and the nation from Margaret Thatcher more highly than the chance to spend another ten minutes in bed? But Downs showed that it was not so simple, and for twenty years scholars have been thrashing rather ineffectively around the paradox he drew attention to.

The problem is that it is unlikely, and we all know it is unlikely, that our individual votes will be crucial. Each voter who is not indifferent between the parties has a 'party differential': the measure of how much more a government of his favourite party is worth to him than one of the next party. This may be a large sum. It is not just that I expect one party to make me richer than another. Governments do many things which citizens value even though they do not affect their pocketbooks. My preference between the parties may depend as much on what they say they will do about abortion or voting rights as on their tax promises. But to compare benefits and costs, I need a common standard for the financial and non-financial benefits, so that I can say (for instance) that I would be prepared to pay £2,000 if that bought me a government led by Michael Foot instead of one led by Margaret Thatcher.

The problem is that this party differential must be 'discounted' appropriately. It must be multiplied by the probability that mine will be the vote that determines which of these governments we have. And that probability, unfortunately, is infinitesimally small. In Britain, it is the combined probability that my constituency will be won by one vote and that the winning party in Parliament will win by one seat. In a US presidential election, it is the combined probability that my vote will swing my state's electoral college delegation and that that swing will change the outcome of the election. Combining independent probabilities means multiplying them. If I think there is one chance in 30,000 that mine will be the crucial vote and one in 300 that mine will be the crucial constituency, the overall probability that I will swing the election becomes $\frac{1}{30,000} \times \frac{1}{300} = \frac{1}{9,000,000}$. There is one chance in nine million that my

voting makes the difference between getting and not getting my
£2,000 party differential; 8,999,999 times out of nine million, it
either arrives even without my vote or fails to arrive even with it. So
the 'expected value' of my vote is not £2,000, but £ $\frac{2,000}{9,000,000}$.
That works out at about 0.02 pence, or two-thirds of the face value
of a single Co-op dividend stamp. If the cost of shoeleather and so
on is any more than that, it is irrational for me to vote at all.

A great deal of energy has been spent in trying to find a way of
avoiding this rather shocking conclusion. Like the debate on critical
elections discussed in Chapter 3, the debate on rational abstention
has produced a lot of sound and fury but not much progress, and I
shall try to summarise it in my own words rather than by quoting
contributions (but see Barry 1970, ch. II and Niemi and Weisberg
1976, pp. 30-1).

One approach is to say that extremely close results are not all that
improbable. In 1966 the Conservatives won Peterborough by three
votes and in February 1974 Labour took Carmarthen from Plaid
Cymru by the same margin. The Republicans gained the US
Presidency in 1876 by one vote in the Electoral College. Labour had
a majority of five in 1950, of six in 1964, and of three over all
parties combined in October 1974 — a majority which it had lost by
1976 in by-elections, so that it depended on pacts and deals with
the Liberals and minor parties to survive until March 1979. Every
extra seat Labour could have won in 1974 would have allowed it to
lose another by-election before being forced to make a pact.
Hairsbreadth results, and even ties, occur quite often in local
elections. Some constituencies, and some states, are marginal and
people know they are; and the polls often make national elections
'too close to call'. The story of the three Plaid Cymru supporters
whose car broke down on the way home to Carmarthen from an
eisteddfod may or may not be true, but there must have been
thousands of voters who realised after the election that if only they
had got their aged grandparents or teenage son out to vote it might
have made all the difference. In marginal areas, the probability of
one's vote being decisive is higher, and citizens realise this. Many
surveys have shown that voters who think the result will be close
are more likely to vote than those who do not. This is hardly a
shattering discovery, but it does confirm one of Downs's predictions.

This does not get us very far, though. Even multiplying our

probability factor by 100 brings the expected benefit of voting only up to 2p. And whereas some constituencies are known to be marginal, others are known to be safe, and there the probability of decisiveness should be depressed, not raised. How then can we account for the 77.5 per cent turnout in Abertillery in February 1974: a seat which had been held by Labour since 1918 and which everybody with the least knowledge of politics would know was safe? The next approach stresses the assorted joys of voting. In some communities, an election is an important social occasion. At a by-election in a Durham mining community in March 1973, the author took to the polls several housebound old ladies who had not been out of the house to see their friends since Christmas. People may also wish to vote for what sociologists call 'expressive' reasons: to express solidarity with their class or community, or gratitude for the privilege of being able to vote at all, for instance.

Much of this lies outside Downs's definition of *political* rationality, though. Suppose I am a warm supporter of Gypsy rights, but know that the Gypsy Rights Party has very little chance of winning the election. It may be politically rational to vote for it nonetheless, to warn my normal party that it must be more sympathetic to gypsies in future if it wants my vote back, or to encourage the Gypsy Rights party to keep trying. But to vote Gypsy Rights just because it makes me feel warm inside is politically irrational. There is a serious risk here of making the economic model empty and tautologous if we broaden and weaken the category of rational actions. I would not do anything unless I got some gain, material or psychic, from it, therefore everything I do is 'rational'. But by explaining everything this explains nothing. Like vulgar Marxism or vulgar Freudianism, a theory which purports to explain everything is unscientific and worthless because there is nothing that would count as a test or a falsification of it. It would really explain nothing at all. For the economic model to retain any bite, psychic motives must be excluded. That is not to say they are unimportant. They are needed to explain behaviour precisely in those cases where the economic model fails. But they should be discussed in another place.

A third approach is to look at factors which increase the benefits of voting by considering its benefits to people other than the voter himself. Downs suggested that one reason why people vote is that they wish to preserve democracy itself, which would collapse if nobody voted, or at least be the prey of tiny, intense extremist groups. Another explanation is that voters calculating their party differentials are thinking not just of the benefits to themselves, but to everybody, from their preferred party winning. Our fervent Labour supporter presumably believes that a Labour government is good not only for him but for everybody else in Britain, or at least most of them. So perhaps his real party differential is not £2,000 but 30 million times £2,000 — a sum that can be multiplied by a very small probability of being decisive and still produce a substantial expected benefit for voting. Note that valuing this sort of 'external preference' is *not* the same as merely getting warm feelings from voting solidaristically with some other group. It is not the voting *per se* that is valued, but the outcome in which the other group benefits. Our altruistic voter values this so highly that it is worth while to vote even with a very tiny probability of being decisive.

But both versions of this explanation are vulnerable to the ancient retort, 'But what if everybody thought like that?' If I know that everybody else is voting to save the system from collapse, then there is no need for me to do so. Of course, if I think that everyone thinks *that,* then nobody else will vote, so I do need to vote. But if everyone gets to that stage . . . The argument seems to flip disconcertingly back and forth, leaving it quite unclear whether I ought to vote or not. There are two or three ways out. One is to say that I have no way of knowing on which side the others will land, so my best guess is that half of them will land on each side. That doubles my expected probability of being decisive (raising it from one in nine million to two in nine million, in our example). Another is to note that in most previous elections quite a lot of people have voted, that there is no reason to expect anything different this time, and that therefore it is quite safe for me to stay at home. It is partly a matter of how risk-averse I am. If I am not just an altruist, but a cautious altruist, I am more likely to vote. The risk that no other supporter of my cause will do so is small, but I don't like taking any avoidable risks.

We have now had our first brush with a paradox that is going to recur again and again in this book, so we ought to face up to it now. It goes under many names: the collective action problem, the public goods paradox, the Prisoners' Dilemma, the Olson problem (named after Olson 1965, a good systematic discussion of it). But these are all names of the same beast, a beast which stalks the forests of political science and often eats unwary campers.

A public good is a benefit which everybody gets, which cannot be divided up and from which nobody can practicably be excluded. National defence is a public good; so is clean air. If somebody builds a navy which sails round and round the British Isles, it protects everybody on the islands, whether they have paid part of the cost of the navy or not. Likewise, it is not practicable to provide unpolluted air for some people in a territory without providing it for everybody else. The preservation of democracy and the return of a Labour government are also indivisible benefits, or indivisible harms to those who do not want them. If anybody gets them, everybody does.

A self-interested rational man considering whether to contribute to the costs of a public good should not ask himself 'Do the benefits of this good to everybody outweigh its costs to me?' He should ask, 'Does *my share* of the benefits outweigh the cost I pay?' If the answer to that is 'no', as it usually is in a large group, he should not contribute voluntarily. In deciding whether to chip in to a collection being taken to pay for the navy, I must guess what everybody else will do. There are three possibilities: (1) if everybody else pays, there will be enough money to build the navy; I will get my protection anyhow because I can't be excluded from it; therefore it is in my interest to be a free-rider on the backs of others; (2) if nobody else pays I would be wasting my money, so there is no point in paying; and (3) if some pay and others do not, there are two possibilities. Either the contributions of the volunteers are enough to pay for the navy, in which case (1) applies; or they are not, in which case (2) applies. I should pay only if, without me, there are just too few contributors to pay for the public good, whereas with me there are just enough. In a group of five this situation arises quite often; in a group of fifty it might arise occasionally; in a group of fifty million it is even less likely than the chance that mine will be the vote which swings the election.

I hope this helps to show why the attempt to break out of the paradox of rational abstention by stressing 'voting to preserve democracy' or 'voting to secure benefits for other people' is a failure. It is an interesting and important failure none the less. We are *not* saying that people do not in fact cast their votes for reasons like these. Of course they do; if they did not, hardly anyone would ever vote. We are not even saying that it is normally irrational to vote. We are saying that the act of voting cannot often be explained within the framework of *economic* rationality of Downs and Olson.

We must go outside the framework to ask questions like 'How and why do people develop ethical views which lead them to disapprove of free-riding?' (see e.g. Mackie 1977), or 'Why do some people become involved in politics even though they get too little remuneration to compensate for their costs?' (see Chapters 6 and 8 of this book). The paradox contains an explanatory success as well as an explanatory failure. It explains why turnout at elections varies substantially with quite small factors. Fewer people vote if polling day is rainy than if it is dry; if it is on a weekday rather than a holiday; if registration is cumbrous and expensive (as in the USA) than if it is simple and cheap (as in Britain); if they have to walk rather than get into a car and ride. Some people have viewed apparently frivolous variations like these with shock and horror. If the economic approach has shown that they are not so frivolous after all, it has achieved something.

POLITICAL PARTIES AND THE DOWNTOWN
SHOPPING CENTRE

The other celebrated and controversial part of Downs's analysis is the theory of 'spatial competition'. The basic principle is very simple and was set out in Chapter 1. To recapitulate, the model suggests that parties wishing to win elections will converge on the middle of the street so that each party is offering a virtually identical bundle of policies, designed to appeal to the median voter. A party which sets up shop anywhere else will lose the election, because the other party need only hold the centre ground to win, and may indeed nestle up towards the extreme party on the majority side of it, in order to win overwhelmingly.

Even this simple model looks like a promising explanation for some real events. In 1964 Barry Goldwater broke away from the middle ground on the right; in 1972 George McGovern did so on the left; both were trounced. (See, e.g. Page 1978). In 1980 Ronald Reagan, previously identified as a distinctively right-wing candidate, moved to the centre very fast as the election approached. He distanced himself from the fundamentalist Christians he had earlier embraced, and convincingly 'won' the final telelvised 'debate' with Jimmy Carter because he was able to brush off Carter's charges that he was a dangerous extremist. That was a long time ago, and anyhow the President misquoted me, implied an easy-going and relaxed Reagan ten days before he won the election.[1]

Nevertheless, the simple spatial model does not capture the whole of voter-politician interactions. It has to be modified to capture some features of the real world and to meet, as far as it can, the objections raised in Chapter 1.

The distribution of voters

The simplest assumption is that voters are evenly spread along the spectrum of opinion in a distribution like Figure 4.1.

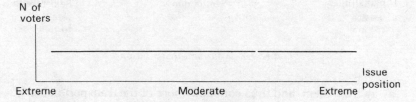

Figure 4.1 An even distribution

A more realistic model for many issues is the bell-shaped or so-called 'normal' distribution, as shown in Figure 4.2, in which there are a few people at either extreme but most are grouped at the centre. The public's attitudes to the distribution of income and, particularly, wealth fit this model.

In this case, the median voter also holds the central position, and the forces pulling the parties to the median voter and the median position are very strong indeed. This helps explain the apparently odd fact that many of the biggest tax subsidies and welfare payments in democracies go not to the very poor but to middle-income groups. Tax relief on mortgage interest, for instance, is a massive transfer away from the poor (who cannot afford to buy houses and therefore don't qualify) and the rich (who have high marginal rates of taxation) to the middle. Transport subsidies are another very popular policy. Small wonder; subsidising loss-making buses and trains out of taxation takes money from the poorest and gives it to the slightly richer, who are more likely both to have jobs and to live further

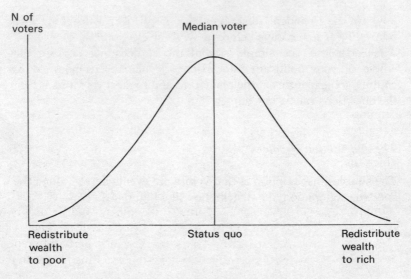

Figure 4.2 A normal distribution

away from them, and thus consume more of the transport subsidy.

However, the median voter does not necessarily hold the median position. Opinion on coloured immigration in Britain in the 1960s and 1970s, for instance, was heavily skewed as in Figure 4.3.

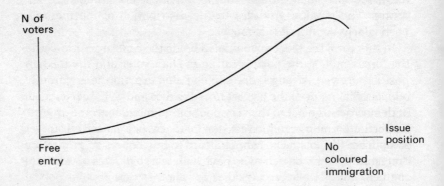

Figure 4.3 An unimodal skewed distribution

In a case like this, it still pays for the parties to support the view of the median *voter*, which is not at all the same as the central *position* of admitting one in every two coloured immigrants who wished to enter Britain. A Downsian party would take a much more restrictive position. And both British parties have now done just that, although they were both initially slow to do so, for reasons that will be examined in Chapters 6 and 8.

Figures 4.2 and 4.3 are examples of 'unimodal' distributions. A mode means a peak; these graphs both have only one peak from which the numbers holding a given opinion slope down steadily on both sides. But opinion cannot always be arranged along a spectrum in such a way that there is only one peak. Figure 4.4 gives a familiar example.

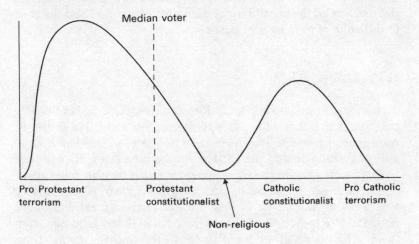

Figure 4.4 A bimodal skewed distribution

Both surveys (Rose 1971) and evidence from elections held under proportional representation (Knight 1974) show that the structure of opinion in Northern Ireland is as shown in Figure 4.4. The Protestant community is bigger than the Catholic, and fewer than one per cent of Ulstermen refuse to identify with one or the other (Rose 1971, p. 248); within the Protestant community voters heavily prefer extremists to moderates when they are forced to make a choice, whereas within the Catholic community the opposite has been the case, although this may be changing in 1981 with the outflanking of the SDLP by the IRA in the two Fermanagh by-elections of that year.

Downs claims that with a distribution such as that in Figure 4.4 the parties will not converge on the median vote, but settle at the two modes. That inference fits Northern Ireland, which is dominated by two extreme Protestant parties (Democratic Unionist and Official Unionist) and one moderate Catholic one (Social Democratic and Labour Party). The parties which have tried to occupy the position of the median voter — a moderate Protestant in this case — have done much less well. However, the inference that in a bimodal distribution parties will settle at the modes, not the median, does not *logically* follow from Downs's initial assumptions at all. To make it follow logically, we need to consider two more features of the real world: the possibility of extremist abstention and the ease or difficulty of forming new parties.

Extremist abstention

The owner of the shop at no. 50 doesn't have to worry about no. 1's complaints that it is a long way to the nearest shop. The family in no. 1 must eat, and so long as it costs less to go to the shop than to start a smallholding in the garden and become self-sufficient they will carry on going to the shop, however much they grumble about it. But it is not the same in politics. Unless there is compulsory voting (as in Australia and Belgium, for instance), extremists are perfectly free to abstain if the nearest party is too far away from them. How strongly does this pull the parties away from convergence? That depends on the shape of opinion and of the propensity to abstain. In an even distribution as shown in Figure 4.1, the pull of the extreme is only half as strong as the pull of the centre. A party which moves one point towards extremism may gain one vote from somebody who would otherwise have abstained. But if the other party follows it in the way the theory predicts, the first party loses two votes to set against the one it has gained. Somebody at the centre will switch from the first party to the second. That costs it twice as much as it has gained from the former abstainer. In the distributions in Figures 4.2 and 4.3 the cost of moving towards extremism is even heavier. In Figure 4.2 each successive issue position away from the centre contains fewer voters than the last; so a party which moves away from the centre to placate extreme abstainers loses *more* than two votes for every one it gains. In Figure 4.3 that reasoning applies to any party tempted to move towards the 'tail' to the left of the diagram, though not to a party tempted to move the other way. What about Figure 4.4? A party which moved from the median (marked with a dashed line) towards the left-hand mode would *gain* more extremists than it would lose centrists, and if the upward slope was steep enough it might gain twice as many or more, thus offsetting the fact that (in the model as developed so far) an extremist may only abstain, whereas a centrist has the option of switching parties. A party moving rightward from the median would have a thin time of it at first (no biconfessional party has ever succeeded in Northern Ireland under the British electoral system) but once established on the uphill slope moving rightwards it would feel the same impetus towards the mode as the left-moving party.

Differential propensity to abstain could add another complication. If extremists at one end were more likely to abstain than those at the other, for instance, that would make the model lean to one side; if they were much more inclined to abstain than centrists, that would pull the parties out whereas the converse would push them in.

The electoral threshold and the electoral system

Real-world extremists have another option. Instead of abstaining, they may form another party. Their chances of success depend crucially on the electoral threshold — that is, the height of the barrier in the way of new parties. In Britain and the USA, these barriers are traditionally very high. No new party has attained national standing since 1918 in Britain (the Labour Party) and 1856 in the USA (the Republican Party). 1981 may yet be the next date on the list with the growth of the Social Democratic Party, but it is too early to tell.

The main reason for the high threshold is well known. It is the plurality, or 'first-past-the-post', electoral system which both countries have. A system which awarded seats in proportion to votes would normally be more generous to breakaways. First-past-the-post penalises splinter parties if their support is dispersed, though it may reward them if it is concentrated. The fate of two breakaway Democrats in the same year — 1948 — illustrates this. Henry Wallace broke from the Truman administration on the left and Strom Thurmond on the right — Wallace disliked Truman's alleged hatred of the Soviet Union and Thurmond hated Truman's alleged sympathy for Southern blacks. Their popular support was identical. Wallace got 1,157,326 votes and Thurmond got 1,176,125. But Thurmond carried four states and won 39 electoral votes, whereas Wallace did not get a single electoral vote. Thurmond's support was concentrated in the Deep South whereas Wallace's was dispersed around the country. In Britain, the Labour Party has never in its life had to worry about the Communists or any other group on its left; there has never since 1945 been a strong enough concentration of left-wing supporters to lose Labour a single seat to them. Labour has suffered more along the regional spectrum than the class one: by October 1974 it had lost three seats in Wales and four in Scotland to the nationalist parties. Plaid Cymru does not attract all that many more votes than the far-left parties; but they are all in the same places: the Welsh-speaking areas where the party can win seats.

Thus in Anglo-American systems parties will suffer from extreme breakaways only if the extremists are geographically concentrated. In proportional systems they may suffer equally from any extreme breakaway, concentrated or dispersed. It does not follow, however, that proportional representation (PR) is good for extremists. In fact the reverse is true: PR harms extremists and rewards centrists. The reasons for this comprise one logical deduction and one further assumption. A move from a plurality to a proportional electoral system lowers the electoral threshold; but it lowers it for everybody, centrist as well as extreme. With opinion distributed as in Figure 4.2 or 4.3, if it is easy for a new centre party to be formed, the others are less likely to move out to placate extremists, because there are far more centrist votes at risk than extremist ones. In 1981 Britain is witnessing a long-delayed centrist revolt with the formation of the Social Democratic Party. Long-delayed in that its founders had ceased to agree with the main policies of the Labour Party years earlier; and in that both the Labour and the Tory parties were offering policies a long way away from the electoral median. But potential Social Democratic voters were very evenly spread across the country, and so a split under first-past-the-post has always carried the risk (and still does) that such a party might get, say, 25 per cent of the votes in the country and not win a single seat. (Ironically, though, if it does better than that and gets 40 per cent in its proposed alliance with the Liberals, it will win almost every seat in the land under first-past-the-post, something which could never happen under PR). If Britain had had PR, the centrist revolt would have taken place many years ago and the Labour and Tory parties would not have moved so far towards their own extreme supporters as they have under first-past-the-post.

The argument of the last paragraph is not valid for opinion distributed as in Figure 4.4. There, the high threshold for new parties under first-past-the-post protects movements towards the centre, unlike the case discussed in the last paragraph, where it has protected movements away. In the late 1960s the leadership of the Ulster Unionist party became much more moderate — partly in a vain attempt to win Catholic votes, but more because it was under intense pressure from the British government to abandon militant Protestantism and make concessions to the Catholics. In 1973 the British government introduced PR in Northern Ireland. The Unionist party promptly split; and the militant wing has totally eclipsed the moderate one. That is what the model, on the assumptions made so far, would have predicted.

Nevertheless, even in Ulster the net effect of PR was to benefit centrists. (That is what the British government hoped for, and why it introduced it. It also explains why Margaret Thatcher will never introduce PR in Britain; nor would Michael Foot or Tony Benn. None of these politicians wants centrism in Britain, whatever they may want in Northern Ireland). To see why, we need to add another assumption to the model: that parties never leapfrog one another in building coalitions, but will only coalesce with parties ideologically adjacent to them. If politics is unidimensional (we shall look at the effect of removing this restriction later on), then extreme parties are inherently weaker than centrist ones. Militant Protestants can only ally with moderate Protestants and IRA supporters with moderate Catholics. But centre politicians could jump either way. The 'power-sharing executive' produced by the 1973 elections in Northern Ireland was in fact a centre alliance which excluded both extremes; and it was brought down not by an election but by a political strike organised by the extreme Protestants. Even a small party like the Northern Ireland Alliance Party, or the German Free Democrats, can have enormous influence if it is at the centre in coalition-building and there is no leapfrogging. Unless one of the blocs on either side of it can gain over half the seats on its own, it will have to be included in every government. And, once a government is formed, the centrist coalition partners still have more power than the extreme ones. For if the latter propose to do something that the centrists don't like, they can threaten to leave that coalition and form another one with the parties on the other side of them. One of the best arguments against PR, indeed, is that it gives too much power to centrists if politics is unidimensional (for more on coalition theory, see for example, Riker and Ordeshook 1973, chs. 6 and 7; Brams 1976, chs. 1 and 7; Abrams 1980).

Ambiguity and abstention at the centre

The next two problems about Downs's model are deeper. As we said in Chapter 1, if convergence brings the parties to exactly the same point, it is hard to see why anyone should bother to vote if, however they vote, they end up with identical governments. Add this to the case for rational abstention discussed earlier and it appears that Downs is the most effective destroyer of his own impressive edifice. The real situation is likely to be more complicated. Parties which strive for the support of particular groups or interests will stress the aspects of their policies which appeal to those groups and play down the aspects which do not. Politicians have a vested interest in ambiguity while voters have a vested interest in clarity. Downs admits that 'rational behaviour by political parties tends to discourage rational behavior by voters' and calls this 'a fundamental tension in our model' (pp. 136-7; see also Page 1976).

There is a clear parallel in the market. Convergent pressures drive most producers of cigarettes or soap powder to make nearly identical products. But they all want to persuade consumers that their identical products are really very different, and they spend millions of dollars saying that X's soap powder washes whiter or that the man who smokes Y cigarettes gets his girl (and rides the handsomest horse). Manufacturers have a rational interest in promoting an irrational decision on the part of consumers.

Maybe this is a comforting conclusion. Capitalism has not collapsed as a result of this contradiction. People have developed a healthy scepticism about advertising claims, and as Schumpeter said a long time ago, 'The most beautiful girl that ever lived never sold a bad cigarette'. Perhaps the same is true of political competition. However, there are differences. For one thing, the consumer (of soapflakes, if not of cigarettes) will always end up buying some brand or other, which is not true of voters. Secondly, I know if I have got a bad cigarette as soon as I light up; I do not know if I have got a bad government until some time has passed, and it is too late to change it for a while. Buying governments is rather like buying from an uninformative mail-order house that refuses to take back faulty or unwanted goods. In general, the dubious claims of advertisers probably do less harm to the integrity of their marketplace than do the dubious claims of politicians to the integrity of theirs (see Brittan 1975 for a pessimistic view).[2]

The problem of multidimensionality

Downs normally assumes that voters' attitudes can be ranked along one dimension, and furthermore that that dimension is the left-right one. This laid him wide open to attack (Stokes 1966) on the familiar grounds that voters do not in fact recognise the left-right dimension. Many writers (e.g. Butler and Stokes 1974, esp. pp. 324-8) proceed by presenting Downs's model as a left-right one, pointing out (correctly) that the electorate does not regard politics that way, and concluding that the spatial model is not to be taken seriously. This is to miss the point, in a rather subtle way. The main limitation of the model is not that it uses the terms 'left' and 'right'. It does not have to, and few of the examples in this chapter do so. The real problem is that it is *unidimensional*: that for simplicity of analysis it assumes that voters bundle up their attitudes on all sorts of questions into ideologies which can be measured along one dimension.

It might seem easy to rescue the theory from this limitation by allowing parties to compete in *n*-dimensional issue space. In two-dimensional space, the situation would be something like that in Figure 4.5. In more than two dimensions, it is possible to have a conception of multidimensional space, even though it is impossible to draw it. In Britain and the USA, issue space is indeed multidimensional. Voters' views about race relations do not fit in

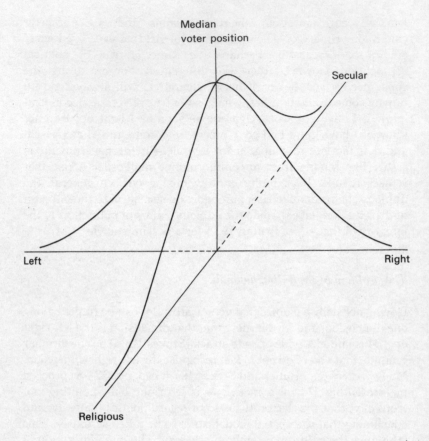

Figure 4.5 Convergence in two-dimensional issue space

any particular way with their views on economic policy, and neither of these fits in any particular way with their views on Northern Ireland. And it is never easy, and sometimes impossible, for politicians to put together policies which capture the middle ground on all of these at once. It may become impossible if the choices on a single decision reflect more than one criterion. A simple example, based on real life, may make this less obscure.[3]

In 1976 Liverpool City Council was divided three ways. None of the three parties — Labour, Liberal and Conservative — had enough votes to control the council on its own, but any pair of parties could win a vote against the third. The parties were not equal in numbers, but, so long as there were no defections, this did not affect their power. A two-party coalition which involved the Conservatives (the smallest party) had neither more nor less power than one which did not. The City Council had to decide what to do with a piece of land it owned. Three solutions were proposed: to landscape it and keep it as public open space; to build council houses (municipally owned housing) on it; or to allow it to be used for private housing. Table 4.1 shows how the parties ranked the options.

TABLE 4.1

PREFERENCE ORDERINGS, LIVERPOOL CITY COUNCIL 1976

	Party:	*Lib*	*Lab*	*Cons*
Order of preference	Best	x	y	z
	Middle	y	z	x
	Worst	z	x	y

(where x = Open Space, y = Council Housing, and z = Private Housing)

If the options are paired off, an odd thing happens: x beats y by two votes to one (we can regard the parties as monolithic voters); y beats z by two votes to one. The condition which economists call 'transitivity', which is one of Downs's criteria for individual rationality, requires that x should therefore beat z. In fact z beats x by two votes to one. There is no alternative that cannot be beaten by another. Note that there is nothing irrational about the *individual* orderings of each party. Readers who know something about Liverpool and something about the ideologies of the British parties will see quite easily how each party arrived at the ranking it did. But individual rationality has led to collective irrationality.

This is 'Condorcet's paradox' or the 'paradox of voting'.[4] It is a special case of a more general problem known as Arrow's Impossibility Theorem which has generated a huge volume of scholarly articles, most of them exceedingly obscure. It is very hard to present in a non-technical way,[5] but, fortunately, that is not necessary for the present argument. The fact that the Liverpool problem was two-dimensional led to an 'Arrow problem' (Downs's terminology: he admits that he 'evades' its implications, in part by making the issue spectrum unidimensional). The councillors not only had to decide whether they preferred open space to housing, but also, and independently, how they ranked council housing vis-à-vis private. That is a relatively simple problem in only two dimensions. Many problems are much more complicated and in more dimensions. The more dimensions which go into ranking options, the more likely 'Arrow problems' become.

Maybe this is all more horrendous in theory than in practice. As we said right at the onset, there are only a few issues on which the electorate has views salient enough to be analysed in a Downsian way. But readers should be aware that the problem exists, and it may mark another of the limits of the economic approach.

THE PROBLEM OF INFORMATION COSTS

A third problem raised by Downs affects both the calculus of voting and the judgment of which party to vote for. Acquiring political information is not costless, any more than voting is costless. As voting takes time and shoeleather, so learning about issues and parties' proposals takes time and usually money. Even if it only costs time, that is an important opportunity cost. While I am reading the Labour Party Programme I cannot simultaneously be reading the poetry of Dylan Thomas; the first activity is costly unless I get as much literary pleasure from it as from the second.

There are two main ways for voters to reduce their information costs. They can use free information which comes their way, and they can get other people to collect and assimilate information for them. Free information comes in two forms: non-partisan and partisan. Democratic governments often try to ensure that as many people as possible are well-informed and actually vote. Not necessarily to ensure that they vote for the party in power, but to ensure that they play their part in keeping the system going. Governments therefore provide their citizens with political information. In the USA, this takes such forms as school civics lessons and official encouragement to people to vote. A British example was the arrangement that the parties imposed on the broadcasting networks, whereby every channel had to broadcast party political messages (shared out among the parties by a formula agreed between the big ones and the TV channels) simultaneously. Only the on-off switch provided an escape until the arrangement was recently modified to let the channels show the party politicals at different times.

Advertising is free partisan information. Of course advertisers are not dispassionate informers. Parties, newspapers plugging a cause, and so on are presenting the information which is most favourable to themselves in the hope that people will support them. Even if they tell no lies, their information is naturally incomplete. Can the voter use this free information without being too much affected by its biases? In the consumer field, it can be done by product-labelling laws. In both countries, food producers must now list the contents of their packages in descending order of weight. This free, though small-print, information is a valuable supplement to advertising claims as we can all find out that there is no ginger in our ginger ale, nor cream in our coffee creamer, and that we all eat more monosodium glutamate, lecithin, and cottonseed oil than we knew there was in the world.

Product labelling laws help consumers (though there remains a puzzle, to be discussed in Chapter 5, as to how they came to be enacted), but there is no real equivalent for political consumers. Fortunately, political consumers benefit more than market ones from 'knocking copy'. Until recently, the convention that the makers of Daz do not directly attack Omo survived in the world of marketing, but it never has in politics. If the Conservative Party fails to advertise the parts of its programme or record that will cost it votes, the Labour Party will.

The other way in which voters can reduce information costs is by having other people do it for them. It is hard for me to decide whether nuclear power really is dangerous or not because I have no scientific qualifications. So I may try to leave an assessment of the risks to the experts: if only I can find enough experts who agree. Or if I am a housewife with young children who has to stay at home, it may cost me less to find out about politics from what my husband tells me his workmates think than to hire a babysitter and go and find out for myself. As with the act of voting itself, the poorer I am the larger the costs are likely to loom. So that when surveys find (as they do) that low-income citizens have a lower turnout and are less personally well-informed than high-income ones, it will not do to infer that they are less rational. They may be *more* rational: husbanding their resources rather than spending them in an area where it cannot make any difference.

There is an obvious drawback, though, to relying on pre-digested information. The person who does the digesting may not have the same values as the person on whose behalf it is done. Relying on an observation such as 'everybody round here votes Labour and always has done because the Labour Party is the friend of the working class' can be dangerous. For all I know, the Labour Party may be merely resting on a reputation, just as the Republican Party from 1865 to the end of the 19th century was content to 'wave the bloody shirt' and remind its supporters about the Civil War rather than actually have any policies. If I went out and assessed the evidence for myself, I might find that 'my' party actually had nothing to offer me. We have already noted that electors' interests in knowing as clearly as possible what the parties stand for conflict with the parties' interest in making it as obscure as possible when it benefits them to do so.

Some famous landmark elections reveal interesting differences on this point. Everyone agrees that some elections changed the course of history: for instance the British General Elections of 1886, 1906 and 1945 and the American Presidential Elections of 1860, 1896, 1932 and 1960. Each of these marked either a decisive repudiation of a party with a distinctive issue position (1886 and 1896 for instance), or the return of an administration which radically changed the direction of public policy, or both. They should all be good tests of the rational-choice argument that voters weigh up the issues before deciding how to vote. But the historical record is patchy, and much stronger on the negative than on the positive side. The voters rejected the Liberals in 1886 and the Democrats in 1896 because they were associated with unpopular stands — Irish Home Rule and 'free silver' respectively. These cases are akin to the rejection of Goldwater in 1964 and of McGovern in 1972. But it is often less clear when the electorate votes *for* radical change. They did in 1860 and 1945, when the issues were clearly articulated and most people knew where the parties stood. The Republicans were against both slavery and secession; the southern Democrats favoured both; the rest were uncomfortably in between. In 1945, the Labour Party was committed to expanding welfare expenditure whereas Winston Churchill and the Conservatives seemed at best to be uninterested. In these cases the voters knew what the parties proposed, knew what they wanted, and voted accordingly. But the other elections on my list are different. In each case, the issue or policies on which the campaign was fought bore little relation to the issues or policies which the winning administration espoused. The General Election of 1906 brought in what was to be Britain's last Liberal government. But nothing that the Liberals did between 1906 and 1915 betrays a party in its death-throes, and quite a lot suggests a party radically changing its traditional policies in response to new demands from the electorate. The Liberals gave trade unions immunity against civil actions by those who lost money through strikes. They introduced the first nationwide, publicly-supported, welfare programme, with old age pensions beginning in 1908 and National Insurance in 1911. They launched employment exchanges and set statutory minimum wages in several industries. All this marks a shift from the nineteenth-century politics of region and religion to the twentieth-century politics of class. But nobody could have predicted that from a study of the election campaign. It was dominated by 'old' issues: free trade versus protection, Chinese labour in South Africa, and the problems of Welsh nonconformists. Even a voter who invested a lot of resources in gathering information would have been unable to predict that once in office the Liberals would, for instance, drop their own proposals on trade-union rights and adopt those of the Labour Party, which were much more radical (see, e.g., McLean 1975, chs. 5 and 6).

The American elections of 1932 and 1960 show a similar pattern. There were *some* radical notes in F. D. Roosevelt's campaign in 1932; a cynic would say that Roosevelt was such an opportunist and cared so little that his statements were mutually consistent that he was bound to sound radical some of the time. His economic message, at any rate, was unmistakably conservative. He accused the outgoing Republicans of being 'the greatest spending Administration in all our history' and that was not intended as a compliment. As Hofstadter (1948, p. 312) wryly pointed out, Roosevelt's famous inaugural appeal, 'The only thing we have to fear is fear itself' was 'essentially the same threadbare half-true idea' as Herbert Hoover's 'bumbling' about the need to restore confidence.

The American election of 1960 resembles the British one of 1906. The Kennedy and (particularly) Johnson administrations broke with the past by vigorously enforcing civil rights and sharply increasing welfare spending. But public debate in 1960 was less about whether there should be a War on Poverty than whether a Roman Catholic could be allowed to become President of the USA. The election was fought on issues of the past which did not presage what the winners would do.

These explorations illustrate some of the strengths and weaknesses of the rational-choice approach. It is at its strongest when it forces us to think about politics in an unusual way and then see how that corresponds to some things which actual politicians and voters do. Politicians do try to offer policies which a majority of the electorate approves of, in order to seek re-election, and in general this procedure does drive politicians towards the centre. Voters do, despite the scepticism of observers in the 1950s, reward or punish politicians according to their closeness to the electorate on the issues of the day.

It is both a strength and a weakness that the 'economic' approach uncovers things which it cannot explain. Its failure to explain why anybody ever votes is an instructive failure: without it students would probably not even realise that there was a problem requiring an explanation. The same applies to the tension between what is rational for a politician and what is rational for a voter. Once we know what needs to be explained, we can go in search of explanations. Various search missions will be undertaken in later parts of this book; the reader will have to judge whether they find anything.

Part II

The Intermediaries

Voters elect politicians; politicians try to implement policies which will get them re-elected. But for most of the time the links between voters and politicians are not as direct as that. On the way up, between voters' views on issues and politicians' decisions on policies, are two important intermediate groups: pressure groups and party activists. On the way back down, between politicians' decisions on policies and the effects which voters can observe, lies an equally important group, the bureaucracy. The next three chapters will examine each of these groups in turn.

5

Pressure groups

What [they] . . . are aiming at is power, and power without
responsibility — the prerogative of the harlot throughout the ages
Stanley Baldwin, 1931, on the owners of the
Daily Mail and *Daily Express*

TYPES OF GROUPS — PRODUCER, CONSUMER, AND ALTRUISTIC

A pressure group is any group which seeks to influence the policies
of government without taking on the responsibilities of government.
This may make them sound no better than Stanley Baldwin's
harlot. Many democratic theorists, from points of view as diverse as
Rousseau, the American Federalists, and Joseph Schumpeter, have
argued that pressure groups or 'factions' distort democratic politics.
Others believe, however, that it is actually essential to democracy
that groups should be allowed freely to come together and campaign
for their political objectives. At any rate, any active attempt to
suppress them would be an enormous restriction on freedom. They
exist, and will continue to exist in any society that can reasonably
be called liberal as well as democratic.

Every scholar who has written a textbook on pressure groups has
produced a scheme for classifying them. Unfortunately, they are all
different. For the analysis in this book, I am going to divide
pressure groups into three categories: producer groups, consumer
groups, and altruistic groups. I do not claim that this is the only
possible classification or even necessarily the best; merely that it is
a convenient way of looking at the differences between groups with
a view to explaining why some succeed and some fail. It is primarily
a classification of groups, not of individuals: one or two individuals
may join, for instance, even the 'purest' of altruistic groups for
impure reasons.

Every group which lobbies the government to do, or refrain from

95

doing, something, must stand in one of three relationships to the policy it desires. Either its members stand to benefit themselves from the policy, or they do not. If they do not stand to benefit, their group is altruistic. If they do stand to benefit, they benefit either in their capacity as consumers of goods and government policies, or in their capacity as producers: controllers (not necessarily owners) of land, labour, or capital. Many pressure groups of course span more than one type. But here are some British examples of very nearly pure representatives of one type.

Producer groups
The National Farmers' Union
The Amalgamated Union of Engineering Workers
The Engineering Employers' Federation

Consumer groups
The Consumers' Association
The Post Office Users' National Council
The National Union of Students

Altruistic groups
The Royal Society for the Prevention of
   Cruelty to Animals
The Lord's Day Observance Society
Oxfam

Each producer group controls what economists call a 'factor of production' and can threaten to stop it from being used. That is what gives them much of their strength. The National Farmers' Union could in principle stop land from being used productively; the engineering workers can withdraw their labour; the employers can bar access to their capital (factories and the equipment in them) or refuse to provide fresh capital equipment. Consumer groups control no factors of production (the National Union of Students cannot meaningfully 'withdraw its labour' because its members are not producing goods or services for anybody else) but are still looking for benefits for their members. Their members and potential members may be everybody, as in the first two examples, or they may be a specific group, as in the third. Members of altruistic groups likewise control no factors of production. But they are unlike consumer groups in that their members are not looking for direct benefits to themselves. (I assume that members of the Lord's Day Observance Society already observe the Lord's Day themselves, and are not hindered from doing so by government or anybody else). They are looking for benefits to *other people,* or animals. Any benefit they get for themselves is only indirect: the warmth of knowing that other people or animals are better off than they would otherwise be.

Obviously, some pressure groups are more successful than others. The National Farmers' Union has had much more success over farm subsidies than the Consumers' Association. The RSPCA gets more money and more protective legislation, on behalf of animals, than most altruistic pressure groups working on behalf of human beings. One generalisation that is often made is that producer groups are stronger than consumer groups; one would also expect consumer groups to be stronger than altruistic ones. But these generalisations are not always true. As I write, twenty-four hours after the murder of John Lennon, one of the USA's most famous, most respected and most feared pressure groups is flexing its muscles: the National Rifle Association, which is opposed to all legislation restricting the freedom of Americans to buy and own guns. The NRA is not a 'pure' consumer group, but it is very nearly so. Its wealth and power come from the majority of its members who own guns, not the minority of them who make them.

EXPLANATIONS OF THE STRENGTH OF PRODUCER GROUPS

Three main explanations of the generally greater strength of producer groups have been put forward. The first is that they are in general the experts in putting pressure where pressure is most effective. In Britain, most government decisions are made by civil servants and Ministers in Whitehall. There, behind the scenes, is the place for a lobbying group which wishes to be influential. French farmers blockade roads with mountains of peaches when they want to complain about the prices they are getting; British farmers negotiate with the Ministry of Agriculture for higher subsidies. In a few cases, but only a few, Parliament is the right place to bring pressure to bear. This applies, for instance, to lobbies on moral matters which are decided on unwhipped free votes in the

House of Commons: abortion, divorce, capital punishment. In these few areas where Parliament does decide, Parliament is the place to go. Pressure on the public, in the form of demonstrations or acts (like the French farmer's and fishermen's blockades) designed to make the lives of third parties inconvenient, are generally regarded as the futile actions of lobbying groups that cannot or will not make themselves heard anywhere more effective.

In the United States the position is similar except for a very much greater role for Congress. Much pressure group activity is on the executive branch, and for fifty years American radicals have complained in particular that regulatory agencies (such as the Interstate Commerce Commission or the Federal Communications Commission) get into a cosy huddle with the industries they are supposed to be regulating. But lobbying Congress is a much bigger and more professional business — complete with paid and registered lobbyists — than lobbying Parliament. The reason, of course, is that Congress makes laws whereas Parliament, in general, does not. Pressure direct on the public plays a relatively small role, as in Britain, and the telephone-bank and mass mailing play a larger part in it than the street demonstration.

This is not, however, a true *explanation* of the strength of groups. It is much more an effect than a cause. It is not that groups become important by lobbying in Whitehall; much more that Whitehall is prepared to talk to them because it recognizes that they are important. Normally, it is easiest for a producer group to win access, because bureaucrats feel that they ought to consult those most involved in a decision, especially if those most involved can make life uncomfortable if they do not like the decision. Incorporating them also makes the decision 'their' decision and transfers some of the costs of enforcing it from the bureaucracy to the lobbying group. If trade unions are brought in to settle a national wage agreement for their members working for the government (the first British politician to incorporate them in this way was Lloyd George in 1915) the government can then leave it to the unions to discipline those of their own members who don't like the agreement. The unions then find that they have bought access to government policy, but at a price.

How do bureaucrats decide which non-producer groups deserve access? This is an important question which has never been properly researched. I can only offer some educated guesses. Two important criteria seem to be representativeness and 'respectability'. An organisation may claim to speak for millions of people, but bureaucrats and politicians may be very sceptical of these claims. The British motoring organisations are a case in point. The AA and the RAC have over seven million members between them and they have launched many campaigns for higher highway spending and lower fuel tax. They were also both opposed to the 'breathalyser' legislation against drunken driving, although the AA later changed its mind. But the Department of Transport does not take these campaigns seriously any longer. It knows that people join the AA to get a free breakdown service, not to express their views on highway policy; and that the motoring organisations often tell the government what their members think but rarely ask their members to tell them (see Plowden 1971, esp pp. 372-6). Many people do indeed suspect the DoT of being a prisoner of the 'highway lobby': but their evidence refers to producer groups (urged on by the lorry manufacturers and the Freight Transport Association the DoT fought for increased axle-load limits for heavy vehicles in the face of unanimous parliamentary opposition), not to the motoring organisations.

'Respectability' also helps. In the field of wildlife conservation, some groups have lined up detailed scientific evidence of the threat from dams or pollution to rare species; others have made dramatic forays in little ships to impede whaling. My impression — and it is only an impression because I know of no systematic studies — is that the first group has been much more successful than the second, because they have persuaded bureaucrats to take their arguments seriously. A British example is the National Centre for Alternative Technology in mid-Wales, which works in both styles. Its experiments on minimum-energy housing and on methane production from human, animal and vegetable waste receive a good deal of government attention; the rather strident literature opposing nuclear energy which it publicises receives no government attention at all. (Of course, there are other reasons besides its stridency for the government inattention: powerful economic interests promote nuclear energy, whereas none oppose energy conservation. The stridency may be a response of desperation rather than an attempt to persuade.)

The argument about access, then, is not truly an explanation of producer group strength; but it contains the germ of one. As we said, one reason why governments take notice of producer groups is that they fear the consequences of not doing so. Producer groups aim to be *monopolists* of their factors of production. The NFU seeks to represent every farmer, the AUEW every worker in the engineering industry, and so on. In any bargaining, a monopolist is in a very strong position. He can say, 'You need my product; you cannot get it from anybody else. If you get it from me, you may only get it on my terms'. Some groups have more monopoly power than others because they are more truly indispensable. There is no substitute for a doctor. Doctors take years to train and the body which decides that they are fit to practise as doctors is a committee of doctors. If doctors threaten a strike, they cannot be replaced by other doctors who are not in the union, nor can the country do without doctors for a few days or weeks. The only restraint on doctors' monopoly power is self-restraint. Fortunately for the rest of us, most doctors most of the time believe that it is unethical for them to strike. Engineering workers are not so indispensable. Much of the history of trade unionism is a history (more successful in Britain than the USA) of blue-collar workers trying to acquire the monopoly power which doctors cannot avoid having. If the union could nominate apprentices and say how many of them there must be on a job, it could control entry to the trade, and ultimately determine how many people possessed the scarce skills and knowledge required of a competent engineer. They could then be monopolists when dealing with employers and governments. But this sort of would-be monopoly is vulnerable to determined strike-breaking, and to technological change which makes the trade skills redundant or less important than formerly. Furthermore, a country can live without engineering products for longer than it can live without medical services.

Unlike producer groups, neither consumer nor altruistic groups control any factor of production. As there is nothing over which they have monopoly control, there is no sanction they can threaten against a government which proposes to reject their suggestions or to ignore them altogether. There is another factor which tends to strengthen producer-groups vis-à-vis the rest. It is a version of the public goods paradox first explored in Chapter 4, and it explains why the key division is not between self-interested and altruistic groups, but between producer and consumer ones. One might expect that groups which want something which will benefit their own members would, on normal assumptions about human self-interest, be stronger than groups which want something which benefits others. But the catch is the public-goods paradox. Many of the things consumer groups press for are classic examples of public goods. They are indivisible and non-excludable. If there is a law requiring manufacturers to list the contents of the packets of food they make, everybody shares equally in the benefits of that law and nobody can be excluded from it. The government can scarcely pass a law saying that those who have contributed to the costs of a consumer lobby may shop in stores where products are fully labelled, but that those who have not are banned from them.

The dilemma for potential lobby members is therefore the same as we explored in Chapter 4. Either I expect that the campaign will succeed even without my help, or I expect that it will fail even with my help. In either case, it is pointless for me to contribute. To the complaint, 'But what if everybody thought like that?' the classic retort is, 'If everybody thought like that, I'd be a damn fool not to'. Only in the very unlikely event that the lobby would fail if I did not contribute but will succeed if I do is it rational for me to contribute. The relevant question for a potential lobby member is not 'Do the benefits to humanity of getting this policy outweigh the costs to me of lobbying for it?', but 'Do the benefits to *me* outweigh these costs?'

Olson (1965) suggested that a successful group was one which could offer selective incentives to its members: benefits which, unlike the public goods the organisation was primarily lobbying for, were divisible and excludable, and could be offered to those who joined the organisation and nobody else. This is a valuable idea, because it explains a lot about how pressure groups (and many, many other bodies) actually work. The Consumers' Association runs a magazine called *Which?* which tells subscribers what products are safe and good value for money. The only way you can find this information out is by becoming a member of the association (unless you borrow or steal their magazines). The magazine is not sold on the newsstands, nor may articles from it be reprinted anywhere else. The association spends more money on running the laboratories where it tests goods than on general public-interest lobbying on behalf of consumers. All this is as Olson's model predicts.

Even producer groups may be hit by Olson's paradox, although they are not hit as hard as the others. When a trade union negotiates a pay rise, it is normally a rise for everybody in the industry, whether they are members of the union or not. To counter this, the union may offer selective benefits (a union-run insurance scheme, for instance, or help for unemployed members who are looking for jobs), or it may try to impose selective harms on those who are not members (calling them names, boycotts, songs, even physical intimidation). The more natural monopoly power such a body has, the more it can use it to coerce its own members, or reluctant members who would otherwise be free riders. It is also true, from both sides of the picture, that small groups of producers are usually stronger than large ones. In a small group, it is more likely that my contribution *is* the one which tips the balance; thus the case for free-riding is less strong. Also, the members of a small group can spot, and take action against, one of a small number of free riders much more easily than can the members of a large group. This model would imply that in Britain the telecommunications manufacturers (there are only three) would have an enormous influence over Post Office[1] policy; that the smallish number of defence contractors would have a large but not so overwhelming influence on the Ministry of Defence; and that the fragmented civil engineering industry would have relatively little influence on the Departments of the Environment and Transport. This prediction seems to fit reality, although the Official Secrets Act will forever loom in the way of any systematic test.

Most producer groups and some consumer groups can survive, then, by offering selective benefits. But this is nothing like a complete explanation of the success of some groups. Altruistic groups, for instance, can normally offer no selective benefits. And even those which can have problems with them. True to Olson's prediction, the National Union of Students held its potential membership together in the 1960s and 1970s by selective benefits: an insurance agency and a travel service. But the travel service collapsed; probably because it was in a competitive market with other organisations which offered selective benefits (travel for those who paid for it) without the overheads of paying the costs of a lobbying organisation. Thomas Cook Ltd does not employ people to negotiate with the government over the level of student grants. And the insurance agency will now accept business from non-students, so that it is no longer a selective benefit. Since these events, the NUS seems to have suffered more from disaffiliation of individual unions than it did before.

If 'selective benefits' will not do the job of explanation, what will? Note, before we proceed, that we are in a similar position to our discussion of 'rational abstention' in Chapter 4. The 'economic' explanation has essentially failed to explain why any non-producer groups exist; but its failure is an instructive failure because it does explain why those that do exist are fewer and (usually) weaker than producer groups. An old-fashioned pluralist would expect there to be as many groups as interests, with membership proportionate to their strength. The Olson theory explains why there are not.

As with the other paradox, the next step is to jump out of the 'economic' framework in its narrowest form. It is not 'rational' for a self-centred egoist to give money to Oxfam, but that does not mean that it is not rational to do so. People are charitable for all sorts of reasons. Hobbes, and some cynical moderns, have wanted to say that all charity is at bottom self-interest; somebody who gives money to a beggar is doing it because he is grateful that he is not in the same position. But psychological egotism of this sort is either false or trivial (see e.g. Peters 1967, pp. 143-9). Some people have selfish political aims, and some have altruistic ones — the latter are not necessarily any less rational than the former. In some situations, it is true, bad motives drive out good. If one person behaves selfishly in, say, exploiting common land or building up an arsenal of nuclear weapons, he may force others to do the same in order to survive, even if they would have preferred to act altruistically. But in matters of less than life and death, altruistic behaviour even in prisoners' dilemmas is commoner, exactly because less is at stake. The stark choices of, say, disarmament negotiations do not face people thinking of volunteering to work for pressure groups.

In any case, as Barry (1970, p. 35) pointed out, the 'leisured and gregarious people' to be found in the Anglo-Saxon upper middle-classes may actually think that time spent in committee meetings has a negative cost. This helps to explain why, ever since the days of Mrs Pardiggle and Mrs Jellyby,[2] lobbies for the welfare of poor people are mostly run by rich people, who unfortunately may have different ideas to the poor's of what the poor want or ought to want. In this, middle-class Marxists are no better than Mrs Pardiggle.

Notice that consumer and altruistic groups are in the same boat; and, significantly, with the same sort of middle-class activist at the oars. The activities of a Consumers' Association activist benefit herself as well as others; those of an RSPCA one benefit only others. But the incremental quantities of benefit that the first one gets for herself as a result of *her own* participation are so small that the activity might as well be considered as purely altruistic.

THE POWER OF PRODUCERS VS THE POWER OF THE VOTE

We have still not eliminated a puzzle. Nothing in this chapter so far, for instance, explains why the National Rifle Association is one of the most powerful lobbies in the USA. Let us look at four cases in which the generalisations of the previous section do not apply: two in which consumer pressure outweighed producer pressure, and two where an intense minority for what they see as a public good outweighs an apathetic majority for whom the same policy is a public harm.

In the Populist and Progressive eras in the USA — from about 1880 to 1920 — the railroads were not popular. Their management was arrogant ('the public be damned' as William H. Vanderbilt said) and often corrupt; and they had a monopoly in carrying goods to market over any distance. As we saw in Chapter 3, popular unrest against the 'robber barons' and other monopolists crystallised in the Democratic campaign of 1896. But it had already won some legislative victories before that. The most important was the Sherman Anti-trust Act of 1890. A 'trust' was the name commonly given at that time to a company which controlled a large part of the business in some product or service — one we would now call an oligopolist or monopolist. Under the Sherman Act the courts were empowered to demand the break-up of trusts so as to provide for competition and prevent them from making monopoly profits. Admittedly, the Act was largely window-dressing to start with. But after 1904 President Theodore Roosevelt appointed lawyers to prosecute antitrust cases, and himself publicised and promoted a show trial of a leading railroad trust called Northern Securities. Antitrust is a prominent feature of American business law to this day.

Many critics have condemned antitrust as all show and no action, but this view is exaggerated (for a good summary of the controversy, see Wilson 1980, ch. 15). The trust busters genuinely did attack *some* trusts even in the early days. In any case, it is still worth asking how the Sherman Act came to be passed at all. For the case contradicts the rule that producer groups outweigh consumer ones in the lobby. The railroads and other oligopolists should have been the strongest sort of lobby: a small, rich one. Their 'victims' should have been the weakest sort: a large, poor one. The antitrust case shows that there is a counterweight to producer group power, and that is vote power. There were more farmers than railroad barons in the American electorate. They had less lobby power but more vote power. Politicians win votes by promising to 'do something' about the grievances of large groups, not those of small ones. This is what happened in both antitrust and pollution control, our next case study.

In both Britain and the USA, 'the environment' was the great new issue of the 1970s. Appropriately the USA, the land par excellence of 'private affluence and public squalor', in J. K. Galbraith's phrase, first of all allowed pollution to get worse than in Britain, and then swung abruptly to more extreme environmental controls. The USA has the most rigorous controls in the world over automobile exhausts. And Federal regulations adopted in 1972 proposed a time-limit of 1985 after which *no* effluent at all would be permitted in American rivers (Wilson 1974, p. 149). As many critics have pointed out (e.g. Tullock 1970, pp. 202-206), a rule which requires manufacturers to return water to the river purer than it was when they took it out and purer than Nature makes the Mississippi or the Rhone is a tough, arbitrary and apparently unfair rule. Pollution problems are almost never dealt with by the economists' proposal of a tax on the polluters or a subsidy for equipment which will reduce their pollution, and almost always by the politicians' proposal of a uniform standard or a blanket ban, even though hydrocarbons from a car exhaust in the Arizona desert have a very different impact on the atmosphere than hydrocarbons from a car exhaust in Los Angeles. In Britain, the most important legislation (the Clean Air Act 1956) takes a more moderate approach. It does not lay down mandatory, nationally-enforced standards, but empowers local authorities to act. Hence, and sensibly, open coal or wood fires are mostly banned in cities where there is too little pure air to absorb their unburnt carbon, but permitted in the countryside where there is sufficient.

Pollution control is a fascinating subject for the student of public goods paradoxes and of lobbying. It is no good leaving it to the market. Everyone knows that clean air is better than polluted air.

However, each individual's decision to burn clean or dirty fuel will make a minute difference to the environment but a noticeable difference to that individual. Clean fuel almost always costs more, and certainly requires more expensive equipment to burn. So a classic public goods problem arises. There is no point in my co-operating unless I know that everybody else will, or will be made to. That is where government comes in. Only government regulation can break this particular public goods problem and introduce pollution control. Perhaps free-market economists such as Gordon Tullock should be a little more tolerant of politicians' efforts. For the wonder is, as Dr Johnson said, not that it is done badly but that it is done at all. Politicians must enact laws on pollution control which favour a large but weak consumer lobby over a small but powerful producer one. As in the antitrust case, this is sometimes possible because vote power counterbalances lobby power. The power of the vote is always latent, but it is not always actual, and somebody has to point out to voters that they would gain from legislation, and to encourage them to vote for politicians who promise to introduce legislation and against politicians who do not. James Q. Wilson (1974, 1980) has suggested that pro-consumer legislation gets passed when political 'entrepreneurs' of this sort have succeeded in making it a vote-winning policy. In order to do so, as we shall see in Chapter 8, they have to evade a rather subtle form of the public goods paradox themselves.

My other two cases are not producer-vs-consumer ones. They are cases where consumer opinion is divided, but where one side has political entrepreneurs who muster votes and the other side has not. The issues are fluoride in Britain and gun control in the United States.

Fluoride is a substance that prevents tooth decay. Some areas have it naturally occurring in their water supplies and others do not. North and South Shields are socio-economically similar towns that face each other across the mouth of the Tyne. South Shields' watei supply is naturally fluoridated whereas North Shields' is not. South Shields children have significantly healthier teeth than North Shields children. This evidence, and more like it, persuaded dentists and others to lobby for adding fluorides to the water supplies of areas in Britain where they do not occur naturally. This has aroused a storm of protest. The two main points on the other side are that fluoride has harmful side-effects (this has never been scientifically demonstrated) and that it is morally wrong to tamper with the public's water supply by introducing 'compulsory medication'.

In recent years, the anti-fluoride lobby has done outstandingly well. Hardly any water authority is now proposing to add fluoride to its supplies and some which did so earlier are now abandoning it (see *The Economist*, 10/1/76). Fluoride is almost certainly a case in which an intense minority confronts an apathetic majority. The few people who are opposed to fluoridation are opposed to it very intensely indeed; the many people who favour it, or who would favour it if they thought about the matter, are not very much interested. This difference translates into a difference in resources and a difference in votes. The antis are prepared to produce and distribute propaganda and to lobby water authorities; the pros, on the whole, are not. Politicians who have to decide on fluoridation know that they will lose votes if they favour it and they will not lose any if they oppose it. So they oppose it. No entrepreneur has succeeded in mustering opinion on the other side.

Gun control in the USA is a very emotive issue. An affection for guns is buried deep in many people's minds in ways which are quite alien to British experience. The Bill of Rights says that 'A well regulated Militia, being necessary to the security of a free State, the right of the people to bear Arms, shall not be infringed.'[3] The West was won by the gun, and Good triumphed over Evil because Gary Cooper was the fastest man on the draw in town. Shooting animals is a popular sport, not an aristocratic preserve as in Britain. Most surveys show that a majority of Americans would favour federal restrictions on the purchase and ownership of handguns. But, as in the previous example, the minority — in this case a large minority — is very intense. Its lobby, the National Rifle Association, fires well-aimed salvoes at Congress every time the issue of gun control is raised. Late 1980 was one of those times, when many Americans were deeply shocked at the handgun murders, in quick succession, of Dr Michael Halberstam and John Lennon. But they have been shocked before: in 1963 at the assassination of John F. Kennedy, and in 1968 at the deaths of Robert Kennedy and Martin Luther King, for instance. And when President Reagan himself was almost killed in a handgun attack in March 1981, the cause of gun control suffered, if anything, a setback. People were impressed less that the President had been attacked than that he had survived, and had shown his true grit by announcing from his hospital bed that he was still against gun control. By projecting himself as a Western hero in fact as well as celluloid, Reagan had made gun control seem almost cowardly and unAmerican.

Up to now, the gun control lobby has thus failed to find its entrepreneur. Wilson suggests that an atmosphere of crisis and scandal helps entrepreneurs on behalf of latent interests. His examples are food and drug legislation in 1906, which followed the exposure of scandalous adulteration of food, and auto safety and emission control legislation, which followed the discovery that General Motors had made a crude and incompetent attempt to compromise Ralph Nader by setting a private detective on him. Likewise, in Britain the clean air lobby surged forward after the London smog of 1952, which not only caused many deaths from bronchial illnesses, but was also a piece of news which Fleet Street could hardly miss. It is possible, though unlikely, that a gun-control entrepreneur may arise in America; the status quo will not change unless politicians decide that there are more votes to be won than lost in gun control laws.

A FORCE FOR GOOD OR A FORCE FOR EVIL?

As we noted at the beginning of this chapter, many early writers on democracy were disturbed at the very notion of pressure groups: they were 'sinister interests' which got between the people and their government and distorted the people's will, often by outright corruption. Two influential academic studies of the 1950s (Mills, 1956; Hunter, 1953) added empirical evidence for the traditional view. Mills claimed that the United States was run by a unified élite of economic, social and military notables, a 'military-industrial complex' which ruled, no matter what President or political party nominally reigned. Hunter claimed to find, similarly, that local business élites dominated the government of Atlanta, Georgia, to the virtual exclusion of the people and the total exclusion of the black people. The leading British semi-academic study of the same era (Sampson 1962) was more sceptical of the 'power élite' theory, but it did contain a famous table (Sampson, 1962, p. 35) showing how many members of the Conservative government were related to the Duke of Devonshire.

These attacks produced a 'pluralist' counterattack, led by Robert

A. Dahl. Dahl and others proved, without much difficulty, that the evidence on which Hunter and Mills rested their case was extremely shaky. In their own empirical studies, they claimed to find 'minorities rule', or what Dahl now calls 'polyarchy'. 'Polyarchy', he claims, is a better term than 'democracy' to describe how countries such as Britain and the USA are actually governed. In most communities, national or local, no one group was decisive over all others. In New Haven, Connecticut, the answer to the question 'Who Governs?' (Dahl 1961) was 'Nobody'. On different issues, different groups were influential and, although the Mayor of New Haven exercised considerable influence, he could not get his way on everything. The best British pluralist study is Hewitt (1974). Hewitt compared the outcome of various disputes in British national politics since 1945 with what the pressure-groups concerned wanted. He found that no group 'won' all the time, or even significantly more often than the rest. One group which did quite well was public opinion. For those issues where there was a meaningful public opinion the outcome went more often than not with the majority.

In parallel with his empirical work, Dahl gradually developed a pluralist political theory (Dahl and Lindblom 1953; Dahl 1956, 1971) which countered earlier theorists' suspicions of pressure groups. According to the new theory, strong groups were evidence of a healthy democracy, or polyarchy. There was nothing sinister about the fact that some groups got their way and others didn't. Either the first had more support than the second, or the support of the first was more intense than that of the second. Providing that those who were in the majority on one issue were likely to be in the minority on another — a likely situation in a complex society not riven by any one huge cleavage — pressure groups posed no threat to democracy.

Pluralism was intellectually dominant in the 1960s and early 1970s; but lately the pendulum has swung back, and it is again popular to condemn 'sinister interests'. The fightback began with those who stressed that there are 'two faces of power' (Bachrach and Baratz 1962). The outcomes of the issues which were discussed did not consistently favour any one group; but what about the issues that *weren't* discussed? Might some group not have the power to see that some things never made the agenda at all? Some proposals might never be raised at all because their proponents knew in advance that they would not stand a chance.

This so-called 'elitist' approach[4] can give a valuable jolt to pluralist complacency. There are clearly issues about which it is true. In 1900 nobody ever argued that the state should make rules restricting property owners from putting up what buildings they wanted where they wanted. In 1981 hardly anybody ever argues that it should not. At both times the excluded option is just not on the agenda. In 1931 the British National Government took the £ off the gold standard, an action which ended the financial panic which had been brewing for four months and had helped to topple the previous Labour government. But as Labour ex-ministers complained with justice, 'nobody told us we could do that'. Until it happened, it was regarded by many key advisors, especially the Governor of the Bank of England, as inconceivable.

Perhaps there are many other cases in which a government and the pressure groups it deals with (including its own bureaucracy) are so used to a traditional way of thinking about the world that they cannot encompass a new one. But a difficulty with 'elitism' is that it is often hard to know what counts as evidence for, and especially against, it. If an élite group is exercising thought control over the rest of us, the fact that they deny they are doing so would not get us very far. A theory which is hard to falsify is problematic; one that is impossible to falsify (Freudian psychoanalysis, for example) is simply unscientific. The 'elitist' view of élite power is not simply unscientific; but the difficulty of testing it can cause serious problems.

The public goods paradox, and Olson's application of it to pressure groups, is another challenge to pluralism. We have seen that there is no reason to expect that all groups with equal popular support will form equally powerful lobbies. The less a group is affected by the public goods paradox, in general the more powerful it will be. The more it lobbies for indivisible and non-excludable benefits the less incentive there is for its potential members to contribute. Furthermore, the incidence of the problem does not lie evenly across society; it falls disproportionately on the poor. The poorer I am the less I can afford the luxury of a political activity to whose prospects my contribution will make no measurable difference. So pluralist group politics may contain a bias towards the rich and powerful. Certainly, vote power may pull the other way to some extent. Aristotle noticed a long time ago that in every society the majority was poor. If democracy meant the rule of the majority, it meant the rule of the poor. (Aristotle, who was not poor, was against democracy). But vote power really benefits not the poorest but the median voter. It softens, but does not cancel, the impact of this public goods problem.

The enemies of pressure groups also claim that they are the main cause of a practice that leads to undesirable distributions of resources, namely logrolling. The US Senate arguably contains not two parties but 100 (and the House of Representatives 435). Each Congressman's claim to re-election depends not on what he did for his country, still less for his party, but on what he did for his district. So, to the dismay of reformers, Congress spends a great deal of time voting highly divisible (and visible) benefits to particular territories: a dam here, a naval base there, disaster relief there. This is derisively called 'pork-barrel politics'. But how does money for a dam in (say) Arizona get through a Senate which, by 98 votes to two, has no interest in it? This is where logrolling comes in. 'I'll back your dam if you back my army base'. Everyone else is in the same boat, in which every individual raid on the pork-barrel would be voted down if people voted straight-forwardly for their direct preferences. So each legislator realises that the simplest way to win money for his schemes is to promise support for projects in which he has no direct interest in return for others' support for his own (see Mayhew 1974, *passim*, esp. pp. 87-91).

Some Congressmen, at least in public, will not admit that any paradox exists. In the 1980 election campaign, I heard one of Virginia's U.S. Senators condemn the Carter administration, in successive sentences in his speech, for allowing public funds to be wasted on inflationary and unnecessary projects, and for failing to provide Federal funds to dredge Norfolk harbour. Either attack on its own might have had some force; together, they sounded a bit incongruous.

Naturally, powerful lobbies for particular subsidies exist, and among the most powerful are those lobbying for protection — that is, protection from competition from imports — for particular industries. Protection is a private good but a public harm. If the government makes it hard for me to buy cheap foreign shoes, by either taxing imports or physically restricting them, then I lose money unless I am in the shoe industry. If I consume shoes, I am being forced to buy expensive home-produced ones instead of having the choice of cheaper foreign ones. If I produce shoes (either as a

worker or as a manager) this drawback is outweighed by the
monopoly profits which I and my fellow-producers can make. It is
not surprising, therefore, that there are strong producer-group
lobbies for protection. If *everybody* is protected, though, nobody
gains an advantage. Everybody must buy native goods they might
not otherwise have bought, and, although producers of each product
do better than foreign producers of the same product, they do not do
better than native producers of different ones. Nevertheless, log-
rolling in the United States in the 1920s and 1930s resulted in the
Smoot-Hawley tariffs, which produced this situation. Every Congressman wished to add the product made in his state or district to
the list of those protected by tariffs. Without log-rolling they would
all have failed; with it, they succeeded.

In a classic article called 'Why the Government budget is too
small in a democracy', Downs (1960) combined the argument about
the public goods problem with the argument about log-rolling to
reach a conclusion which is actually more subtle than his title. It is
not just that the government budget is too small; rather, that the
government spends too little on indivisible public goods (like national
defence) and too much on divisible goods (like army bases in the
districts of persistent or powerful congressmen). The benefit I, as a
voter, get from having a navy is not obvious. It would only become
obvious if my country was successfully invaded because it did not
have a navy. On the other hand, the cost — taxation — is much
more obvious. If a naval base is built in the next town, however, the
benefits to me are much more tangible. The local economy profits,
and so do I. I am willing to pay taxes for that. Unfortunately, log-
rolling means that many other towns are getting naval bases too,
and so I am not getting a bargain for my tax money after all. An
optimist would conclude that the effects of these two paradoxes
cancel out. However, there is no guarantee that the best national
defence arises from locating facilities in the home districts of the
most powerful politicians.

The debate in Britain is less about log-rolling than about
something labelled 'corporatism'. Log-rolling happens in Britain as
well, as any student of, for example, the regional distribution of
subsidies to the steel industry will confirm. However, it is much less
prominent in British than in American politics. This is because
party discipline exists and the separation of powers does not. Once
the government has decided on a particular public spending policy

it is virtually certain to be able to implement it in the shape it wishes to. It does not have to worry about pressures from backbenchers, on its own side or the other, to change the programme in order to benefit their localities. Academic concern about 'corporatism', however, has existed at least since Beer's (1965) well-known study. Beer argued that the political traditions of the past — he called them Old Tory, Old Whig, Liberal, and Radical — had become submerged in a new collectivism that was common to both the Labour and the Tory Party. One feature of collectivism was 'functional representation'. This was the theory that the people ought to be represented according not just to where they lived, but also to what they did. Workers had a right to be consulted as workers; managers as managers, farmers as farmers and so on. Functional representation has historically had a broad appeal. It appealed to Guild Socialists in the early 20th century and to Tory opponents of the Reform Bill of 1832. It also fits pluralist ideas about a government run, democratically or 'polyarchically', by 'minorities rule', and the instinct of politicians and civil servants to consult those a decision will affect before making it, and indeed involve them and their members as far as possible. A good example is Denis Healey's budget of 1976, in which he promised tax cuts which were conditional on the TUC holding trade unionists to a certain stipulated maximum annual wage increase.

That is functional representation — or, to its enemies, 'corporatism'. What do they have against it? Stripped of rhetoric and utterly misleading comparisons with Mussolini's Italy, their case is that corporatism is undemocratic. Eleven million workers are in unions affiliated to the TUC; but about the same number are not, and many decisions taken in co-operation with the TUC affect not only the eleven million TUC-affiliated members, but the entire twenty million plus workforce, or indeed the forty million plus electorate. What right, the critics say, does the government have to go into a huddle with the other estates of the realm — typically the TUC and the CBI — and take decisions which affect everybody? Pressure groups, as we saw earlier in this chapter, do not represent all members of society equally effectively; they represent the rich better than the poor, and producers better than consumers.

The critics of corporatism have perhaps become too alarmed. The history of corporatism shows that it comes and goes, rather than that it has increased, is increasing, and ought to be diminished.

Take, for example, the incorporation of trade unions in British government decision-making. This had a modest start in 1911, when authorised unions became agents of the government in running approved National Insurance schemes. It sped up enormously during the first world war, when the government needed the unions' help in running war production efficiently and in supplying manpower to be killed in Flanders. Union representatives appeared on official committees and a Cabinet Minister (first Arthur Henderson, then George Barnes) who was a trade unionist was appointed.

After 1918, though, the movement went into reverse. The government no longer needed the unions, and the unions lost their influence. They did not regain insider status until the Second World War, when they became indispensable again for the same reasons as during the first. They were courted by the Attlee and Churchill post-war governments far more than by the governments of the 1920s, but their elevation to estate of the realm status did not come until the Conservatives' conversion to 'planning' after 1961. From then until 1979 (except for a sticky patch between 1970 and 1974) union-government co-operation ran smoothly. However, there has been another reversal since 1979. The Thatcher administration is consciously rebelling against corporatism; and, at a time of the highest unemployment since the 1930s, the trade unions are finding not only that the government no longer wants to talk to them, but that they have no way of making it listen.

Nor does this story apply only to trade unions. The CBI — the traditional 'peak organisation' of employers — is not much closer to the inner counsels of the Thatcher government than the TUC. And the rise of consumer groups, notably environmentalist ones, has been almost as dramatic in Britain as in the USA. Environmentalists play no part in a corporate state.

CONCLUSION

Pressure groups are here to stay. Some of the arguments in this chapter may read as if I am siding with the long line of critics of 'special interests' since Rousseau. That is not my intention; the trouble is that phrases like 'seeking power without responsibility' and 'log-rolling' have picked up pejorative connotations. This should not imply that those who do these things are evil. Their actions sometimes have evil consequences. Not as often as pressure-group critics maintain, because group power is balanced by vote power. But not never either, as some pluralists maintain. However, evil consequences do not imply evil actors or evil motives. Log-rolling, for instance, has consequences which are bad for everybody, although nobody intended them. But to condemn lobbyists for pressing for their special interests, or Congressmen for agreeing, is simple-minded, and to rein in their activities without severely curtailing freedom of speech and association could be hideously difficult. The best-laid schemes of mice and men gang aft agley.

6

Party activists

I had a cousin, a young man who didn't take any particular interest in politics. I went to him and said: 'Tommy, I'm goin' to be a politician, and I want to get a followin'; can I count on you?' He said: 'Sure, George.' That's how I started in business. I got a marketable commodity — one vote.

George Washington Plunkitt, 1905

Many people would never dream of becoming party activists. Many thankless tasks are involved: going out on cold wet nights to canvass for votes, with a chance of meeting abusive voters or aggressive dogs; attending long meetings in draughty halls on uncomfortable seats; endlessly trying to think of new ways of raising money, and so on. It is no surprise that relatively few voters take any part in politics beyond voting. Only 14 per cent of Butler and Stokes's British sample, for instance, were conscious of being members of a political party; only three per cent had helped in a General Election campaign; and only 0.3 per cent had held some local party office. (Butler and Stokes 1974, p. 21).

But a cup that is three-quarters empty for some people is a quarter full for others. Three per cent of the British electorate means nearly a million people; 0.3 per cent means nearly 100,000. Common sense is enough to explain why most people are not activists; it is not enough to explain why some people are: more than, say, listen to Radio 3 on an average evening. In this chapter we shall look at three sorts of activists, labelled Non-Ideological Entrepreneurs, Ideological Entrepreneurs, and Expressivists. The last group, as the name implies, are active for what sociologists call 'expressive' reasons: the activity itself gives them some gratification. The others have an 'instrumental' orientation. They join to achieve some ulterior objective. For them, the party is a means, not an end. Of course, real activists may combine two or all three motives for joining; but it is helpful to consider each separately.

116

NON-IDEOLOGICAL ENTREPRENEURS

George Washington Plunkitt was almost a pure example of this type (Plunkitt 1963). Tammany Hall was the headquarters of the Democratic Party in New York City in the late 19th century. To its opponents, such as the Progressive reformers, it was a byword for corruption. To its friends and sympathisers, both at the time and since, it was a mediator between the newly arrived immigrants and the harshness of city life without welfare services. Plunkitt was a loyal and typical staffer of 'the organisation'. He was an Irishman from a poor unskilled background who worked his way up the hierarchy of Tammany Hall by trading in votes, favours and services rendered. As the quotation at the head of this chapter makes clear, Plunkitt was cheerful and explicit about what he was doing and why, and his book is a delight (though it is uncertain how much was actually written, or said, by Plunkitt and how much by his journalistic 'ghost'). To the people further up the organisation he offered votes. In return, he got some favours for his clients and took his profits in the form of favours for himself. At eleven he was a butcher's boy; at 48 he was building docks and harbours; he died a millionaire at 82. It was, he insisted, 'honest graft', not 'dishonest graft'. Engaging in petty fraud such as accepting bribes from people who wanted jobs was not only dishonest; it was unnecessary and foolish. The real advantage of being an insider (Plunkitt held a string of city and state offices culminating in a term as a State Senator) was information: on where the city was about to buy land, for instance, so that Plunkitt could get in for himself and resell to the city at a handsome profit. 'He seen his opportunities and he took them': that was Plunkitt's epitaph on himself. His techniques apply to Edinburgh and Dundee in the 1960s as much as to New York in the 1890s. Information is what insiders have and the rest of us have not. Some people value secrets just because they are secret — this would be an example of an 'expressivist' reason for activism. Others want to know in advance where the city is going to buy land or let contracts. Many local authorities, in both Britain and the USA, have got strict rules to try to prevent insiders from turning their information into cash. But it is impossible to legislate against the use of inside information, as George W. Plunkitt well knew.

Information and hence wealth were the benefits: what were the costs? Time was the biggest. Being a Tammany politician was more than full-time job. Plunkitt's 'ghost' kept a record of the boss's day. It started at 2 a.m. with a trip to the police station to bail out a saloon-keeper. After a few more hours' sleep, Plunkitt heard fire engines passing his house. He immediately got up and followed them to the fire — fires 'are considered great vote-getters' — and arranged for clothes and food for those made homeless. The morning was spent arranging the release of drunks, the discharge of debtors, and the rehiring of sacked municipal employees. At 3 p.m. Plunkitt 'attended the funeral of an Italian as far as the ferry' where he had to abandon the cortège in favour of a Jewish one. And so on, unremittingly, till midnight.

Only a few marshals and brigadiers in the Tammany army held public office. All the other ranks, from the footsloggers to the junior officers, operated only in and through the party. They were purely party activists, of a sort sometimes found in Europe as well as in America. A recent study of politics in Donegal, for instance, aptly showed why it was the Irish who made the most of Tammany Hall. (Sacks 1976). In Donegal, Fianna Fail politicians bought their voters' loyalty in cases of stout, council houses, road-mending jobs, and posts in the party itself. This last was a curiosity. Irish politicians have much less real patronage to dispense than American city bosses. Irish local government is largely run by county managers with very little answerability to the county council. The unspoken reason for this is that it protects officials from pressures to give houses or jobs to the clients of councillors. But it means that much of the 'patronage' that councillors or TDs (members of the Irish parliament) have consists merely of posts in the party itself — the body which is supposed to dispense patronage. The status this confers is mostly symbolic, and belongs more in the 'expressive' section of this chapter.

Britain is closer to Donegal than to New York City. Being a party activist can produce some, but not many, tangible rewards. There have been times (Poplar in the 1920s, Walsall in 1980-1) when local authorities have openly decided to give preference in employment to people who were declared political sympathisers of the party controlling the council. Far more often, it has been widely suspected but not proved that party members were more likely than non-members to get jobs as school headmasters or caretakers.

One other area where party influence is admitted is in the appointment of JPs — that is, unpaid magistrates. The parties regularly send lists of nominees to the secret committees that advise the Lord Chancellor on JP appointments. If you want to be a JP in South Shields, you should do conspicuous good works in the Labour Party; in rural Oxfordshire, make that the Conservative Party and in rural Wales make it the Liberals.

But even a magistrate, though he gains status and power from his position, does not gain money. The powers of patronage available to British politicians are strictly limited because most public service jobs are competitively recruited by professional administrators; houses are allocated on 'points systems' by council officials and not by councillors (the behaviour of Protestant councillors in Northern Ireland before housing administration was taken from them in 1972 shows why not); and 'exceptional needs payments' from the Supplementary Benefits Commission have taken the place of buckets of coal from self-interested philanthropists (when anything has). In New York, Plunkitt was right, from his point of view, to bewail the 'curse of civil service reform'. In one of his glorious perorations,

> I see a vision. I see the Civil Service monster lyin' flat on the ground. I see the Democratic party standin' over it with foot on its neck and wearin' the crown of victory. I see Thomas Jefferson lookin' out from a cloud and saying 'Give him another sockdologer; finish him', and I see millions of men wavin' their hats and singin', 'Glory Hallelujah!' (p. 89).

In Britain, there has never been so much patronage, and it is not always possible to restrict what there is to members or even supporters of the party.

There is a quite different, but still non-ideological, motive for party activism. Barber's (1965) well-known study of Connecticut State legislators divided them into Spectators, Advertisers, Reluctants, and Lawmakers. It is the Advertiser who concerns us now (we shall look at the others later). One of Barber's Advertisers explained himself as follows (p. 69):

> . . . a lawyer cannot advertise. The only way that he can have people know that he is in existence is by going to this meeting, going to that meeting, joining that club, this club, becoming a member of the legislature — so that people know that there is such a person alive.

And they figure that — 'Oh, X, I heard of him. He's a lawyer. Good, I
need a lawyer. I don't know one. I'll call him.'

Lawyers are the most obvious case. In both Britain and America,
their professional associations explicitly ban them from advertising.
So the best substitute for advertising is doing lawyer-like things in
the public eye: eloquent speeches, successful advocacy. Other
professions (accountants, doctors) also have advertising bans, but
politics is not quite so directly useful to a doctor as to a lawyer.
Except when his fellow-members fall ill in the assembly, he has no
equivalent visible way of plying his trade. After lawyers, small
tradesmen have most to gain from being advertisers. Smith the
butcher, who is on the Council, will get free coverage in the local
paper; Jones the butcher, who is not, will have to pay for his
advertisements.

Advertisers usually have no particular commitment to the party
as such. Barber's Advertisers were intolerant of any form of party
discipline. In Britain, a would-be advertiser must take the party
much more seriously, because of course the political parties exercise
considerable control over who is elected, both locally and nationally,
and a little control over what they may then say and where they may
say it. But there is no question about it: the party is a means, not an
end.

IDEOLOGICAL ENTREPRENEURS

When somebody asked Boss Richard Croker of New York what he
thought about the 'free silver' controversy of 1896 (see Chapter 3),
he replied, 'I'm in favour of all kinds of money — the more the
better.' (Quoted in Plunkitt 1963, p. 88). Croker was in the same
party as William Jennings Bryan, but he was not in it for the same
reasons. When we speak of 'party activists', we think much more
often of a Bryan than a Croker. That is right, because the Bryans,
whether or not they outnumber the Crokers, certainly contribute far
more to the style and internal politics of their parties. The most
obvious of all motives for joining a party is the hope of influencing
its policy, and of helping it to come to power so that its policy may
become the nation's policy.

In Britain, party activists of this sort can be traced back to the late 19th century. The idea of an election manifesto was not new. Robert Peel had announced his programme, called the 'Tamworth Manifesto' from the name of his constituency, for the General Election of 1835; Gladstone's Midlothian Campaign of 1879-80 forcibly outlined the anti-imperialist foreign policy he would pursue if the Liberals were elected in 1880; Joseph Chamberlain's 'Unauthorised Programme' of 1885 was a list of domestic social reforms on which Chamberlain campaigned in the 1885 General Election. All of these examples, however, lacked two characteristic modern features. They were manifestoes of individuals, not parties (as the title of Chamberlain's makes explicit); and nobody pretended that active party members had any say in drawing them up.

The real precursor of modern manifestoes was therefore not any of these, but the Liberals' Newcastle Programme of 1891, drawn up at the annual conference of the National Liberal Federation held in that city. The Newcastle Programme committed Liberals (or so their enemies claimed) to a number of highly radical policies which many parliamentary Liberals disliked, and the role of non-parliamentarians in making Liberal policy was actually cut back in later years. As we noticed in Chapter 4, the great reforming government of 1906 was not elected on a great reforming manifesto, or on any clear manifesto at all. After the First World War, the Liberals never succeeded in reconstructing their grass-roots organisation to provide either policy or finance, a failure to which some writers (e.g. Cook 1976, chs. 7 and 8) give considerable weight in discussing the Liberal collapse in the elections of the 1920s.

Meanwhile, Joseph Chamberlain had defected to the Conservatives and taken his organisation with him. Lord Randolph Churchill had already tried, for his own purposes, to involve grass-roots party members in Conservative policy-making. So in the Edwardian years, the Conservatives were probably giving their members outside Parliament a bigger say than the Liberals in policy-making. While Lord Salisbury was party leader (1885-1902) he would have no truck with it; but he was succeeded by his indecisive nephew A. J. Balfour (who once wrote a scholarly article called *In Defence of Philosophic Doubt*). By now Joseph Chamberlain was a single-minded enthusiast for protection ('Tariff Reform') and used the National Union of Conservative and Unionist Associations to put pressure on Conservative MPs and the latter to put pressure on

Balfour, even though Balfour was 'puzzled greatly' as to how to conduct a meeting to find out what Conservative MPs thought. As far as he knew, it had never been done before (see McKenzie 1964, pp. 68-76). Since then, the Conservatives' Annual Conference has always discussed policy, though it has never persuaded the party's leaders that they have a duty to take instructions from it.

Both the Liberals and the Conservatives started with a parliamentary group which begot a grass-roots organisation. With the Labour Party, it was the other way round. The party was brought into existence at a 1900 conference of trade unionists and socialists, which voted 'to devise ways and means for securing the return of an increased number of Labour members to the next Parliament' (see e.g. McLean 1975, 1980). Therefore the Labour Party Conference, which makes arrangements for candidates to stand for Parliament under the Labour flag, also claims the right to decide the policy of every branch of the Party, including the parliamentary one. This claim has rumbled on controversially through the whole history of the party, and played a large part in provoking the split of 1981. When the 'Gang of Four' formed the Social Democratic Party in March 1981, therefore, they did not intend that the party outside Parliament should instruct its MPs on policy. On the other hand, they did claim at their foundation Press conference that theirs would be the 'most democratic' party in which every member would have a direct and equal voice in making policy. The claim has of course not been tested yet.

In the USA, activists have had much less say in party policy-making. Ironically, this is largely the work of a group of people who earnestly wanted to raise the moral tone and ideological content of American politics — the Progressives of the years 1896-1920. The Progressives dearly wanted to sweep away the city machines of Boss Croker, George Washington Plunkitt and their like. In the end, they succeeded. They cut out the gangrene from American party politics. Unfortunately, the surgery killed the patient.

The most important innovation was the primary election. This took the nomination of candidates away from party caucuses and gave it to the people, or at least to all party members (for a more detailed description of the varieties of primary from 'closed' to 'wide-open', see any textbook on American government.) But in getting rid of the bosses this move got rid of all party discipline of any sort. As we have already noticed, anyone who is rich enough (or can persuade enough people to finance him) can set up in business as a Republican or Democrat, whatever his views on policy. In the 1980 elections, the author spent some time watching the Senate contest in Colorado, where both main candidates exemplified this. The Republican was not popular with the state Republican party, possibly because they thought she was too liberal. They refused to put her name on the primary ballot; she fought that decision in the state courts and won. The publicity helped to give her victory in the primary and very nearly gave her victory in the election. The Democrat was a prominent liberal — he had been campaign manager for George McGovern in 1972 — who was expressing unorthodox views that were both the product of genuine conviction and highly diplomatic in a conservative Rocky Mountain state. He appealed to his fellow-Democrats to find 'a new path to old goals':

> Market forces, rather than government allocations, should dictate personal economic choices. The elderly and disadvantaged must be buffered against the shortfalls in a leaner society, not through government handouts but . . . by non-bureaucratic instruments.[1]

Asked whether these views had got him into trouble anywhere, he made it clear that there was no body, and since Lyndon Johnson had ceased to be Senate Majority leader in 1961 no individual, who had any power at all to discipline a Democratic US Senator[2] (even Johnson had cared nothing about members' views. For an excellent description of Johnson's methods, see Kearns 1976).

While many British commentators deplore the strength of party discipline over candidates, some American ones long for some. This perverse little fact became clear around 1900, and again around 1950 when the American Political Science Association sponsored a report called 'Toward a More Responsible Two-Party System' (APSA 1950). This called for two main changes: parties should tell the electorate clearly what they intended to do, and they should involve their active members in drawing up their manifestoes (there is a useful summary of the report in Ware 1979a, pp. 70-74). The APSA wanted the American parties to get to the position the British Liberal party had reached in 1891.

It would have been unrealistic to expect much to happen without fundamental political and even constitutional changes. But there have been some tentative moves towards activist involvement in

American party politics. The 1968 Democratic national nominating convention in Chicago was an undignified mess in which one of the last 'bosses', Mayor Richard Daley, was accused of fixing the nomination of Hubert Humphrey inside the hall while his police were bludgeoning anti-Vietnam war demonstrators outside. Before the 1972 convention the party set up a commission to look into the selection of delegates. It found that 'blacks, women, and young people' were 'significantly lacking in representation', (quoted in Kirkpatrick 1975, p. 265) and instituted changes that ensured that these groups were represented in the 1972 convention in about the same proportion as they comprised in the population. The effect of this was to shift power in the convention from non-ideological activists to ideological ones — from Boss Croker to W. J. Bryan.

In some states — Wisconsin and Colorado for instance — the Democrats were also trying to get some activist control over policy-making. In Colorado, they held an elaborate series of precinct, city and statewide meetings to hammer out a Democratic programme for each level of government (Ware 1979a, ch. 6 and 1979b). The pyramid of meetings resembled the procedure by which resolutions for the British Labour Party Conference work their way up from individual wards and union branches to the Conference agenda. The Colorado meetings continue, and there seems to be more activist involvement in Democratic policy-making there than almost anywhere else in the USA.[3] But the fatal gulf has not been bridged. There is no more of a mechanism than there ever has been for ensuring that lawmakers, or would-be lawmakers, pay any attention to the platforms that are so elaborately constructed. At national level, this cruel truth was exposed by the total failure of attempts by the Democratic National Committee to discipline Democratic candidates for office who were lukewarm in supporting the proposed Equal Rights Amendment.

ACTIVISTS: 'THE MOST ADVANCED MEN'?

For the entire century in which ideological entrepreneurs have claimed a share in policy-making, many politicians have regarded them with alarm. In 1877 the Liberal leader, Lord Hartington, complained that Joseph Chamberlain's National Liberal Federation might put power into the hands of 'the most advanced men'. On the other side, Lord Salisbury thought that the National Union of Conservative and Unionist Associations was bound to be controlled by the 'militants and the wire-pullers who were not representative of the Conservative opinion in the country as a whole'.[4] These fears were most elaborately voiced and documented in a massive academic study (Ostrogorski 1902). Ostrogorski claimed that representative democracy was being undermined by unelected caucuses who were demanding the right to impose their views on MPs and replace them by more amenable candidates if they did not submit. The Newcastle Programme was for Ostrogorski what the Labour Party conferences of 1980-1 were for the founders of the SDP.

Most modern evidence shows that Hartington, Salisbury and Ostrogorski got their facts right, though the facts are of course neutral: in themselves, they imply nothing about what *ought* to happen. On the evidence of everybody who has studied the question, party activists are more militant than party leaders. A typical recent survey, for instance (Whiteley and Gordon 1980) found that Labour conference delegates were light-years away to the left of Labour voters (they were also much more middle-class). The marxist Militant Group was the strongest faction, and Tony Benn was easily the most popular future leader, among the delegates; Labour supporters at about the same time would have preferred Shirley Williams, who had not yet made herself unavailable by changing parties. Labour activists are to the left of the PLP and of inactive Labour voters; Conservative ones are to the right of the Conservative Party in Parliament and probably also of Conservative voters as a whole. The position of Liberal and SDP activists is less clear, for reasons which will be analysed later. Richard Rose, it is true, summarises his study of all this with the claim that 'attitudes towards questions of policy are more or less randomly distributed among constituency parties and, it may be assumed, among party activists as well' (Rose 1976, p. 209); while Tony Benn introduces a recent book containing interviews with constituency activists by challenging 'the media' for 'dismiss[ing] the constituency delegates as unrepresentative extremists' (Jenkins 1980, p. 9). However, both claims are embedded in evidence which contradicts them (only one of Jenkins's 40 interviewees, for instance, expressed views which were distinctively to the right of the consensus of activists, and even she was probably more radical than the median Labour voter) and

TABLE 6.1

DEMOCRATIC IDENTIFIERS VS. DEMOCRATIC NATIONAL CONVENTION DELEGATES, 1972

	Busing		Compelling welfare recipients to work		Rights of accused	
	Identifiers	Delegates	Identifiers	Delegates	Identifiers	Delegates
Left wing position	15	66	22	57	36	78
Neutral position	6	9	9	15	14	9
Right wing position	82	25	69	28	50	13
	*	100	100	100	100	100

Source: Kirkpatrick (1975), Tables 1, 2 and 3.
* This column adds up to 103: this is claimed in the source to be a rounding error. (The full tables have seven categories, here collapsed into three). The options offered were 'bus to integrate' vs. 'keep children in neighbourhood schools'; 'abolish poverty' vs. 'obligation to work' and 'protect the accused' vs. 'stop crime regardless of rights of accused'. In each case, those agreeing with the first alternative are assigned to a 'left-wing position'.

the conventional view that activists are relatively militant emerges little scathed.[5]

The situation is similar in the USA. Kirkpatrick (1975) compared the views of delegates to the 1972 national nominating conventions with those of ordinary voters who identified with the party. On the Republican side, where no efforts had been made to get a 'representative' delegation, delegates' views on policy were substantially similar to Republican voters'. On the Democratic side, where immense care had been taken to get a 'representative' delegation, the outcome was wildly *un*representative of Democratic voters' views. Table 6.1 shows the width and depth of the gulf.

1972 was of course the obverse of 1964, when the Republicans had learnt the electoral cost of nominating a candidate who appeals to activists rather than to the electorate. In 1980, Ronald Reagan gratefully accepted the money and campaign efforts of far-right and Christian fundamentalist activists, but as the election approached he kept his distance from them and as soon as he had been elected bitterly disappointed them by supporting neither their men nor their measures.

The empirical evidence that, in Anglo-American two-party systems, party activists are more extreme than elected representatives should not be a surprise. It is exactly what can be predicted from the Downsian model set out in Chapter 4. If the distribution of opinion fits any of the models from Figure 4.1 to Figure 4.3 (flat, normal, or skewed unimodal) it pays any office-seeking party to move towards the issue position of the median voter, and even under the bimodal distribution of Figure 4.4 it may do so. Where does this leave the party activist? Let us look again at Figure 4.2, assuming for graphic convenience that we are describing one of the issues, such as the distribution of wealth, where voters really are normally distributed from left to right.

Figure 6.1 is designed to illustrate the tensions that are bound to cause strain inside office-seeking parties. A party has to choose between tending to the centre (to maximise the prospects of winning the next election) and tending to 'its' extreme (to stop its activists from becoming disaffected). Whichever route it chooses, it is bound to disappoint very many people. There is no escape from that.

But why are we assuming that activists are 'bound' to be extreme? Because the model implies so. Consider the position of somebody debating whether to join, say, the left party. That decision has

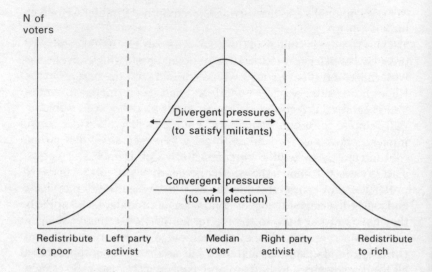

Figure 6.1 Party activists and the normal distribution

costs; if he is not an 'expressivist' he will join only if the costs are outweighed by the benefits. The free-rider paradox discussed in Chapters 4 and 5 has already shown us that this is a tough test. Our potential party member must have one of three policy views. He is either to the right of the median, on it, or to the left of it. The voter to the right of the median will obviously not consider joining the left party, assuming that the parties do not leapfrog around. Will the voter on or around the median? No again. He knows that electoral pressure is likely to push the parties towards the policy he favours without any action on his part. If he can get what he wants without paying for it, why on earth should he pay? The case for free-riding is overwhelming. By contrast, the voter to the left of the median sees the same facts from a different perspective. If he takes no action, the party will drift towards a policy he opposes. Only by becoming active and trying to get the party to accept his policy does he have any chance of bringing it to pass.

The argument is of course symmetrical for a potential right activist. The two arguments may be collapsed together into an even simpler formula. The voter who is on-median has no incentive to become a party activist; the voter who is off-median has. Moreover, the further off-median he is, the more his personal gains from activism are likely to offset his personal costs, and the more likely he will be to prefer activism to free-riding. Thus in a two-party system, there is a quite general tendency for activists to be extreme (see also Robertson 1976, esp. pp. 31-33.) Hartington and Salisbury were both right.

ACTIVIST-PARLIAMENTARIAN STRUGGLES IN BRITISH POLITICS

The previous section shows why these struggles have been so prolonged and so painful. In the Conservative Party, they have endangered the position of two leaders, and in the Labour Party they have provoked three major constitutional crises between 1907 and 1981.

Between 1902 and 1906 Joseph Chamberlain converted almost all the Tory rank-and-file, and most backbench Conservative MPs, to protection. Arthur Balfour tried vainly to hold his government together, but lost Hartington (by this time the Duke of Devonshire) because he had leaned too far towards protection and Chamberlain because he had not leaned far enough. The party went into the 1906 election on the activists' platform, and was decimated by the electorate who had been persuaded that free trade meant 'the Big Loaf' and protection meant 'the Little Loaf'. Nevertheless, Balfour was still pursued by the Chamberlainites and patched up a show of unity with Chamberlain at a party meeting attended by over 600 peers, MPs, and defeated candidates. Even the last, it seems, were not inclined to blame their defeat on Tariff Reform: an eyewitness said that 'Mr. Balfour appeared somewhat in the character of a captive, it being the general belief that he had yielded at the last moment in consequence of the pressure put upon him by numerous members of the party' (quoted in McKenzie 1964, p. 73).

Battered by this experience, Balfour leant much further towards the activists and away from the electorate during his next crisis — over the 1909 Budget and the reform of the House of Lords (the best account of which is still Jenkins 1968; originally published in 1954). Balfour and Lord Lansdowne (the Tory leader in the Lords) urged the Tory peers, who needed no urging, to reject the 1909 Budget. They did, precipitating a constitutional crisis and a general election in which the Liberals could triumphantly proclaim that the will of the people had been thwarted by '500 men, ordinary men chosen accidentally from among the unemployed' in Lloyd George's phrase. The outcome was a Liberal victory in an election which the trend of by-elections suggests the Unionists would otherwise have won. Modern analysts (Blewett 1972, pp. 76-82; Murray 1980, pp. 217-22) have attributed ingenious reasons of various sorts to Balfour, who seems to have known that he was throwing election victory away, but Jenkins (pp. 95-98) was probably right to stress his wish to become aligned, unequivocally, with the party in the country after the long trouble over Tariff Reform.

By July 1911, Balfour was not prepared to go down the same road again. Many Tory peers were urging rejection again — this time of the Parliament Bill, which was designed to curtail the House of Lords' own powers. Balfour would not agree, and was again attacked by his own militants. He resigned the Conservative leadership in November 1911. 'I think the restlessness in the Party, particularly outside the House, has affected him', said Austen Chamberlain with magnificent understatement (quoted in McKenzie, 1964, p. 82.)

The other Conservative leader to get into serious trouble with the party outside Parliament was Stanley Baldwin. Conservatives are not kind to leaders who lead them to electoral defeat, which Baldwin did twice, in 1923 and 1929. In 1930 and 1931, therefore, he faced a sustained attack from the right. Furthermore, he made no secret of the fact that he was prepared to co-operate with the Labour government over a wide range of issues, and would have no truck with the diehardry of 1910-14. The two disputed issues were protection again — now labelled 'Empire Free Trade' — and India, where many activists were perturbed at Baldwin's willingness to concede some limited self-government. Baldwin came very near to resigning, and was saved only by the incompetence of his opponents Lords Rothermere and Beaverbrook — proprietors of *The Daily Mail* and *Daily Express* respectively. In 1930 Rothermere had demanded the right to vet Baldwin's Cabinet appointments if the Conservatives won an election, and Baldwin was able to retort that 'A more preposterous and insolent demand was never made on the leader of any political party. I repudiate it with contempt.' A year later, when Rothermere and Beaverbrook were backing a breakaway 'United Empire' candidate, he rounded on them with the memorable phrase that had actually been suggested by his cousin Rudyard

Kipling: 'What the proprietorship of these papers is aiming at is power, and power without responsibility — the prerogative of the harlot throughout the ages.' Though one of his hearers commented 'Bang goes the harlot vote!' the official Conservative won the by-election and Baldwin's future was secure. The President of the National Union growled to its 1934 Annual Conference that it 'was not called for uttering sweet nothings into Mr. Baldwin's ear but that we might tell him home truths'. But it did not.[6]

The equivalent struggle in the Labour Party broke out in 1907. Keir Hardie had got the founding conference of the Labour Party to agree that its object was to secure 'a distinct Labour Group in Parliament, who shall have their own whips, and agree upon their policy.' This formula made it plain that policy-making was to lie with Labour MPs. By 1907, however, many activists had become very uneasy at Hardie's handling of the female suffrage question, and the Labour Party conference in that year carried a resolution calling the proposal Hardie supported a 'retrograde step'. To the dismay of conference, Hardie abruptly announced that he would resign rather than accept a motion 'intended to limit the action of the Party in the House of Commons'. His overreaction (the motion did not propose to limit anybody's action) led to some hasty fudging, but did not settle the question of who had the right to make Labour Party policy. Some have always argued that the Party chose, sponsored and financed parliamentary candidates; that those elected got in not because of their personal qualities, but because they bore the label 'Labour'; and that therefore Conference and the National Executive were entitled to decide on policy and ask Labour MPs to carry it out. Clement Attlee, as Labour leader in opposition, endorsed this view ('The Labour Party Conference lays down the policy of the Party, and issues instructions which must be carried out by . . . its representatives in Parliament and local authorities'); as Labour Prime Minister, he equally explicitly rejected it, writing to the chairman of the NEC:

> You have no right whatever to speak on behalf of the Government. Foreign affairs are in the capable hands of Ernest Bevin. His task is quite sufficiently difficult without the embarrassment of irresponsible statements of the kind which you are making . . . a period of silence on your part would be welcome.[7]

War broke out again in 1959. Hugh Gaitskell was convinced that Labour had lost that year's General Election because voters thought its class image and commitment to nationalisation were out of date. His left-wing opponents thought Labour had lost because it was not socialist enough and had failed to put its nominal programme to the electorate. Rounds one and two went to the activists; round three to Gaitskell. In 1959 Conference rejected his attempt to delete the party's official commitment to the public ownership of 'the means of production, distribution and exchange'. In 1960 it voted for unilateral nuclear disarmament, in the face of Gaitskell's impassioned and scornful warning that most Labour MPs opposed the policy and would refuse to be corralled 'like well-behaved sheep' to support it. Gaitskell then carried out his promise to 'fight and fight and fight again', and got the decision reversed at the 1961 Conference.

Gaitskell confronted his left-wing critics; his two successors ignored them. Under Harold Wilson and James Callaghan, the Labour Party in Parliament and in government drifted ever further away from the party activists, who passed resolutions criticising the leadership in Conference almost every year. Callaghan, who was Party Treasurer for much of the period, was slightly more sympathetic to the activists than Wilson, but the gap was so wide by the time he became leader in 1976 that even he could not avuncularly bridge it. Not surprisingly, activists began to demand more control over the policy of the parliamentary leadership. In 1970, for instance, Conference carried against Wilson's opposition a resolution deploring the PLP's 'refusal to act on conference decisions'. Its mover pointed out that he and others did many thankless things for the party: 'collecting subscriptions on cold winter's nights, arguing politics on the shop floor, organising and attending countless Party meetings'. But the 1964-70 Labour Government had taken a number of actions in flat contradiction to Conference decisions. Did not members have a right to feel aggrieved? (Labour Party 1970, pp. 180-5).

For the 1979 General Election, Callaghan totally ignored the draft manifesto produced by the NEC and fought the election essentially on a manifesto produced in his office (Bish 1979). This helped bring the old dispute to a head in 1980, when left-wing activists proposed three constitutional reforms to Conference. They were: that the NEC should have sole control over the General

Election manifesto, instead of sharing it with the leader; that all sitting Labour MPs be required to face a re-selection conference in each parliament; and that the electorate for the leadership should be widened to include constituency parties and trade unions as well as MPs. These proposals were designed to make Labour MPs more accountable to the activists, and Callaghan fought them all, especially the first. In October 1980, Conference rejected the first proposal but carried the other two. In January 1981 a special conference at Wembley decided that votes for Labour leader should be allocated to affiliated unions, constituency parties, and Labour MPs in the proportion 40:30:30. In the first two sections votes would be cast by delegates in blocks — each section would be a mini-electoral college. A proposal from David Owen, in his last speech to a Labour Party Conference, for 'one man, one vote' for all party members was heavily defeated.

Wembley has broken up the uneasy Labour coalition, probably for ever. The right-wing 'Gang of Four' immediately set up the Council for Social Democracy which turned itself, with great panoply, into the fully-fledged Social Democratic Party on 26 March 1981. In the months leading up to its formation, the non-existent party was getting a steady 25 to 35 per cent support in the opinion polls. If it forms an alliance with the Liberals, it is likely that it will at least hold the balance of seats at the next General Election. If its 1981 opinion poll support were sustained — a very uncertain proposition — it would win an overall majority in conjunction with the Liberals.

The fate of the SDP will be much clearer soon after this book is published than it is as it is written. At the time of writing, it looks like the most important party breakaway since the Liberal Unionists in 1886. It is a centrist breakaway not an extreme one such as the Communist Party (early 1920s) and the New Party (1931); and it is an extra-Parliamentary as well as a Parliamentary movement, unlike the Lloyd George Liberals (1918) or the National Labour and National Liberal parties (1931). It seems to illustrate that the Downsian argument of pp. 127-8 above needs elaboration. We argued that 'the voter who is on-median has no incentive to become a party activist; the voter who is off-median does'. However, if both parties in a two-party system go off to the ends of the street to satisfy their activists — undoubtedly the position in Britain in 1981 — the situation may be different. Then, for the first time, the on-median voter has an incentive to participate. Free-riding will no longer do if Downsian pressures are not in fact succeeding in bringing the extant parties towards the median. Sufficient voters seem to have felt this to raise 43,500 members and £400,000 in dues for the SDP within eight weeks of its foundation, according to its own claims. This may bring a future government back to the median in one of two ways; either by the SDP-Liberal alliance winning an election, or by at least one of the old parties moving back towards the median to prevent that. If the latter happens (and it may) SDP supporters might still get their policy in even if they fail to get their party in.

Most discussion of activist-parliamentarian relations has been highly value-laden. Most historians and political scientists who have written about the events discussed in this section appear to be centrists; therefore they think that Balfour and Baldwin and Gaitskell and the Gang of Four were right, and their opponents misguided. They have tended to ignore the fact that the militant activist has just as respectable an argument on the other side.

It goes something like this: 'We are the people who endorsed you and whose work put you where you are. We did it because we want to see some policies enacted. Therefore we are entitled to expect you to work for them. If you are not prepared to work for them, you should not have stood as a candidate for this party.' This is not the sort of dispute where one side is right and the other wrong: it is one in which the two sides have incompatible notions of an 'essentially contested concept', representation. So long as the basic pattern of centripetal politicians and centrifugal activists persists, so will the tension between the two. The SDP may escape. It has promised its members a direct policy-making democracy, where all members may vote on party policy (something neither the Labour nor the Conservative party provides for). If it and its members are hovering around the electoral median, the gap between election-winners and conference-resolution-winners may not open up. But again it may, both because voters are keener to support spending programmes than the means to pay for them, and because of the problem of multidimensionality. It may be impossible for a centrist party to be centrist on every issue at once; even if not, there may be no bundle of policies that cannot be beaten by another. The founders of the SDP are committed to keeping Britain in the EEC and to multilateral disarmament. What will happen if the majority of its members are not remains to be seen.

EXPRESSIVISTS

So far in this chapter, we have considered only those who join a party because they want something out of it — money, power, or the chance to influence public policy. A brief word in conclusion is needed on those who join a party just because they want to be members of the party. This is the sort of action that is irrational in Downsian terms, but not necessarily so in more everyday sense of the word. The British parties, for instance, serve all sorts of social functions. The Young Conservatives used to have a formidable reputation as the best marriage bureau in town. Their advertising made great play of their social functions and very little of their political ones. Or, if I live in a picture-book village, I may find that the only way to get in to admire the Squire's garden is by attending a Conservative fête there. In many areas where the Labour Party still has a healthy individual membership, it can be traced to the existence of a thriving Labour Club whose members must also be members of the Labour Party. In earlier days, activists tried to make the Labour Party into a more all-embracing social organisation, partly because life was like that in those days and partly in emulation of Continental social-democratic parties. In Austria, Germany and Holland, for instance, the parties set up networks of subsidiary organisations — socialist choirs, socialist stamp-collecting clubs — so that the party member could live his whole social life under the umbrella of the party. The columns of any pioneer socialist paper, such as the Glasgow *Forward,* are full of the doings of such bodies. Every summer Sunday afternoon in the 1920s, the Glasgow Catholic Socialist Society went on a country ramble from a suitable tramcar terminus.

This sort of thing has waned. Not because the parties no longer satisfy the political aspirations of the people, but because they are no longer needed for their social aspirations. If I want a marriage partner, I can go to a computer dating bureau or on a package 'singles' holiday. If I want to go for a country walk, I can get in my car and go. Today's private lives are much more private — for better and worse — than those of a generation and two generations ago.

A purer form of expressivism is the wish to join the party to express, literally, one's feelings: feelings of solidarity with one's class, sympathy with the underdog, or whatever they may be. People join in order to 'do their bit', or because their relatives fought to preserve democracy in the last world war. Motives of this sort can underlie voting and they can also underlie party work. People want to say that they had a share in the victory, or at worst that they helped to mitigate the defeat.

> And gentlemen in England now a-bed
> Shall think themselves accurs'd they were not here,
> And hold their manhoods cheap whiles any speaks
> That fought with us upon Saint Crispin's Day

as Henry V tells his troops before Agincourt. The author has been a political activist for many years, not to mention a loyal member of the Campaign for Real Ale. For almost as many years he has known perfectly well that it would pay him to be a free rider and either get the benefits without paying or at least not throw his subscriptions away on an unsuccessful cause. He remains prepared to pay a few pounds to good causes rather than become a gentleman in England now a-bed.

7

Bureaucrats

My Minister's room is like a padded cell, and in certain ways I am like a person who is suddenly certified a lunatic and put safely into this great, vast room, cut off from real life and surrounded by male and female trained nurses and attendants. When I am in a good mood they occasionally allow an ordinary human being to come and visit me; but they make sure I behave right, and that the other person behaves right . . .

Richard Crossman, on becoming a Minister, October 1964

'Bureaucratic' is a handy term of abuse. Bureaucrats are probably less popular than anybody else discussed in this book. They are very commonly criticised, first, for being inhumane, inefficient and rule-bound, and, secondly, for usurping the power that should belong to elected governments and the people who elect them. Only the second criticism is central to this book, but a preliminary word is needed on the first, so that they can be distinguished from one another.

Our everyday encounters with bureaucrats are with junior clerks in front offices, or on the telephone, or replying (late) to letters of complaint. In this light, bureaucrats are not very attractive people: distant, unsympathetic and not too bright. When my local tax office kept sending me letters in red threatening to send the bailiffs in unless I paid some tax that in fact I had paid months earlier, I did not fall in love with bureaucrats. For me, it was important; for them, I was just another aggrieved member of the public. Some of them justifiably aggrieved, some not; but it is not the job of the counter clerk to judge which is which. The most important fact about a routine bureaucratic job is just that it is routine. No large organisation — public or private — can delegate to its junior staff the job of deciding whether its rules are appropriate to each case they meet. 'Don't blame me — I don't make the rules' is an infuriating response to the infuriated citizen. But it is hard to see how else a

137

large organisation could be run. The clerk himself knows that he may be promoted if he diligently applies the rules, but he risks serious trouble if he tries to be creative with them. If he is lucky, he may be rewarded; if unlucky, he may be sacked or demoted. The safe — 'maximin' — thing to do is always to work rigorously and unimaginatively to the rules. If the rules are silly, that is someone else's problem.

Many people who curse 'bureaucrats' in this sense also make the ancient mistake of blaming the messenger for the message. They attack those who carry out the policies when they should be attacking the policies themselves. Take planning permission for example. Every so often in Britain, an old age pensioner (it is always a pensioner) is told that she must demolish her newly-built bungalow, into which she poured her life savings, because she failed to apply for planning permission. These stories are a gift to sub-editors, who can clear the front page for tear-jerking accounts of the cruelty of faceless, heartless bureaucrats. But there is another side to the story. The modern land-use planning (zoning) system in Britain dates back to the Town and Country Planning Act 1947, which has been accepted as a basis for development by every government, of both parties, since then. The 1947 system requires local authorities to decide what land should be zoned for housing, industry, open space, agriculture and so on. Most politicians, of both parties, have felt that it was more important to prevent 'haphazard' development — housing in agricultural areas for instance — than to allow owners unfettered rights to do what they want to with their land. The electorate has supported that objective; or at any rate, it has failed to oppose it. The objective has to be enforced bureaucratically, as it cannot practicably be enforced by market or other non-bureaucratic mechanisms. This entails a set of rules requiring people who wish to build bungalows to apply for planning permission, and a set of local officials to enforce the rules. Anyone who objects to a heartless planning officer requiring an elderly lady to pull down her bungalow must be saying either 'I agree with planning rules but object to their bureaucratic enforcement' (which is illogical unless the critic can suggest some other way of enforcing them) or 'I disagree with these rules and think that property owners should be free to do what they like with their property' (which is not illogical, but is a political argument and ought to be addressed to the politicians who make policy, not the routine bureaucrats who enforce it).

When we move from routine officials to top-level ones, however, the arguments are quite different. Nobody ever accuses routine officials of making up the rules as they go along (although some people accuse them of failing to do so); but very many people believe that senior officials do so. That is why they are getting a chapter to themselves in this book. If there is any substance in the widespread suspicion of senior bureaucrats, then they are important intermediaries in politics. Politicians do what they think the voters want (sometimes they do what they think the voters ought to want). But their actions, as mediated by bureaucrats, may look very different to their intentions.

THE REAL RULING CLASS?

The tone of exasperation in which we normally discuss 'bureaucracy' has always been there, ever since the term was coined in mid-18th century France where, it was complained, 'our Masters of Requests refuse to understand that there is an infinity of things in a great state with which a government should not concern itself' (quoted in Albrow 1970, p. 16. Chapters 1 and 2 of this book are a very useful history of the concept). But the exasperation has often been mingled with admiration. Max Weber, the most-read of the classical sociologists of bureaucracy, spoke of its 'indubitable technical superiority' (Gerth and Mills 1948, p. 224). Superiority to what? Weber contrasted bureaucracy with 'traditional' and 'charismatic' authority, and also, elsewhere in his work, with administration directly by amateur or professional politicians — country gentlemen or party regulars. 'Traditional' authority meant authority of a tribal chief or medieval king, who was obeyed because he and his forebears always had been obeyed. 'Charismatic' authority meant authority exercised by somebody who could dominate other people by sheer force of an outstanding personality. Rule by notables or professional politicians was erratic and liable to be distorted by favouritism. None of these was as 'rational' (one of Weber's favourite words) as a system in which officers were recruited by competitive examination, drew a fixed salary, were promoted on merit, and owed their right to give orders to legal rules, not to their social status or personal magnetism.

J. S. Mill was one of many eminent Victorians who could not decide whether bureaucracy was a good thing or not. Competitive examinations were introduced for entry to the British Civil Service after the famous Northcote-Trevelyan Report of 1854, and these reforms were modelled on parallel ones for the East India Company (effectively the top-tier government of India) for which Mill himself had worked. Mill was, not surprisingly, an enthusiast for Northcote-Trevelyan:

> The practice of submitting all candidates for first appointments to a public examination . . . would probably be the best plan under any system; and under our parliamentary government it is the only one which affords a chance, I do not say of honest appointment, but even of abstinence from such as are manifestly and flagrantly profligate. (Mill 1972, p. 342.)

As this shows, Mill worried about the threat to efficiency from democracy. Elected public officials were liable to be corrupt or incompetent. Mill was particularly scornful about the practice of electing judges in some States of the USA. He would have pointed to G. W. Plunkitt as evidence for the superiority of bureaucratic city administration to city-boss rule.

But Mill also felt that bureaucrats were almost bound to become the real rulers of any country in which they emerged:

> A bureaucracy always tends to become a pedantocracy; . . . and it requires a popular government to enable the conceptions of the man of original genius among them to prevail over the obstructive spirit of trained mediocrity. Only in a popular government (setting apart the accident of a highly intelligent despot) could Sir Rowland Hill have been victorious over the Post Office[1].

Where Mill could not make up his mind, it is not surprising that many other commentators could not either. The debate revived only with some modern writers' extensions of rational-choice analysis to bureaucracy (Tullock 1965; Downs 1967; Niskanen 1971, 1973). They argue that bureaucracy is needed to provide some services that markets normally cannot (Downs 1967, ch. IV). For instance, left to themselves, motorists would continue to pollute the atmosphere of Los Angeles with petrochemical smog because nobody has an *individual* incentive to buy costly anti-pollution devices for his car, still less to walk or cycle the many miles required to get from anywhere in Los Angeles to anywhere else in Los Angeles. This is of course the good old Prisoners' Dilemma once again. On this view, the justification of bureaucracy is the justification of government itself. It can and should intervene in cases of 'market failure': stopping Californian motorists from polluting their own atmosphere, for example.

But this immediately raises the prospects of market failure of a different kind, if bureaucrats are devoted not merely to the public interest but to the advancement of themselves and their bureaux *per se*. The literature is rather poor at specifying what bureaucrats actually do try to maximise. Is it their bureau's budget (Niskanen 1971, p. 38)? Not always, as the story of Sir Peter Carey and Mr Tony Benn will soon show us. Is it a quiet life with the fewest disturbances? Is it a tall narrow promotion pyramid with good chances of an exalted title; is it inflation-proofed pensions? No doubt all of these and others; at any rate, their interests are not identical to their employers'. This is no more startling in itself than Adam Smith's comment that we get bread and meat not because of the kindness of the butcher and baker but because of their self-interest. However, the rational-choice writers do not believe that laissez-faire is best for everyone (not when they are talking about bureaucracy, at any rate). Are they right? The best test is to look at the most intensively researched bureaucracy in the world: the British Civil Service.

PHILOSOPHER-KINGS OR OBEDIENT SERVANTS?

'England was the slowest of all countries to succumb to bureaucratization', said Weber[2] — behind France and Prussia, let alone ancient Egypt or China. But the Northcote-Trevelyan recommendations were accepted very quickly, and they have shaped the British Civil Service for a century and a quarter now. Future administrators are selected from the best field of arts (though not of science) graduates applying to any large British employer. They undergo a tough and ruthless screening process involving written examinations, interviews and an exercise in which candidates are asked to prepare a brief for a Minister on an imaginary, but plausible, problem. (The procedure is described in detail by Kellner and Crowther-Hunt 1980, ch. 6, which would-be mandarins should study very carefully indeed; though it may soon be changed in another attempt to remove its alleged biases). Most of those selected are put in a 'fast stream' of jobs with similar pay and titles but vastly different functions to those of other graduate administrators. A 'high-flyer' may be given a job, in his late twenties or early thirties, in the private office of a minister or top civil servant: his first taste, mostly vicarious but tempting, of real power. By his mid-thirties, he can expect to be in the grade of Assistant Secretary, in which he starts making policies rather than applying them. If he is marked for the top, he may then be seconded for a while from the spending department in which he has been working to one of the central ones — the Treasury or the Cabinet Office — before returning to the same department or, increasingly likely as he becomes more senior, to a different one. Out of ¾ million British civil servants, the only ones with a say, or a prospect of a say, in policy-making are the tiny group of 1,700 Assistant Secretaries and above who have been recruited in the way just described. For its admirers (largely outside Britain) the system is a model of how the best and the brightest are recruited and trained into the finest bureaucracy in the world — its only possible rival being in France. For its detractors (largely in Britain) it is a model of how a small unrepresentative group with immense power can obstruct the policies of the elected government of the day. At the moment, the detractors have the best of the argument. In 1980-81, they have even got an award-winning TV comedy series, *Yes, Minister,* on their side. In *Yes, Minister* the devious and disloyal Permanent Secretary, Sir Humphrey Appleby, always gets the better of the well-intentioned Minister, Jim Hacker, except for a wish-fulfilling Ministerial comeback in the last episode. The series has been highly praised for its factual accuracy, and has quarried its plots from many recent exposés such as Richard Crossman's Cabinet diaries and Leslie Chapman's tales of everyday life in the Property Services Agency (Crossman 1975, Chapman 1979). What are the detractors' charges, and what is the evidence?

Policy

This attack comes mostly from the left, though some of the critics (e.g. Sedgemore 1980) believe that civil servants can and do obstruct any radical government, including the Conservative ones of 1970 and 1979. Senior Civil Servants, the argument runs, are disproportionately recruited from 'public' (i.e. private) schools and Oxford and Cambridge, and hence are overwhelmingly of upper-middle-class and upper-class backgrounds. Once recruited, they assimilate — and it is in the interests of their careers to assimilate — the ethos of the service and the attitudes of their department. The department will foster a policy or, at most, a restricted range of policies, and will do everything it can to obstruct a government which wants to do something outside that range.

There unquestionably is a recruiting bias for elite civil service posts. Disproportionately many of those selected are from independent schools and Oxbridge, and once selected the Oxbridge candidates do better than the rest (Kellner and Crowther-Hunt 1980, ch. 6). Even if one accepted all the Civil Service's defences — that Oxbridge produces the best graduates anyhow, that the tests are scrupulously designed to eliminate any class bias, that the Service works very hard to encourage more non-Oxbridge graduates to apply — the inescapable fact remains that senior civil servants are unrepresentative of the people they govern by virtue of both their class and their regional origin. It may not be the Civil Service's fault. Perhaps they select the best of those who apply; and they reject 'quotas' or 'positive discrimination' on the grounds that their job is to pick the best men and women for the job, not put right the wrongs of British society. But, for as long as most of the good applicants come from two universities whose students are disproportionately from public schools and — probably more important but far less often noticed — disproportionately from south-eastern England, for so long will the worries persist.

It is the next link in the argument that is the weak one. The critics have established that mandarins are socially unrepresentative, but not that that implies anything about mandarins' views. If their class background makes them hostile to left-wing governments, why did Kim Philby and Anthony Blunt, who were upper-class Cambridge recruits to the Civil Service, become Russian spies? A subtler version of the criticism may be valid. A bureaucracy tends to attract people who believe in bureaucracies. Those who do not are unlikely to apply for jobs in them. This bias, if it exists, may well have a regional dimension. People who live a long way away from the central government may have less faith in the ability of central government to solve their problems than people who live close to it. Therefore the regional bias in the recruitment of civil servants *may* be important, though of course it is impossible to measure. (In the context of devolution, discussed below, it is important to notice that the Scottish Office does not conform to the pattern set out in the last paragraph; it recruits mostly Scots, and largely graduates of the Scottish universities.)

What about policy matters? From the innumerable examples of civil service obstruction of the government of the day that are tossed around, a few stand out as better documented than most. In 1909 the Treasury were appalled at Lloyd George's Budget proposals, which they thought were dangerously radical. They tried hard to whip up opposition to the Budget wherever they could, inside or outside the Liberal Cabinet (in 1909, unlike now, the Cabinet was allowed to discuss the Budget). The Treasury, 'steeped in the Gladstonian tradition' in Asquith's phrase, had obstructed Chamberlain's protectionist campaigns in 1903-6, but that was a mere skirmish. The activities of its Permanent Secretary, Sir George Murray, against his Minister amounted to open insurrection, as when he wrote to Lord Rosebery in December 1908 pleading for the House of Lords to reject the forthcoming Budget:

> I cannot believe that your House will swallow the Budget if the mature infant turns out to be anything like the embryo which I now contemplate daily with horror. (Quoted in Murray 1980, p. 123.)

As we have seen, the Lords needed no urging. When the Leader of the Opposition and the Permanent Secretary to the Treasury are both urging people of limited intelligence to act unconstitutionally, it is easy for them to believe they are saving their country.

In modern times, two recurrent complaints are that the Foreign Office concealed their calculations of the probable costs of membership of the Common Market from both Labour and Conservative Cabinets between 1967 and 1973 and that the Department of Industry systematically subverted Tony Benn, as Secretary of State in 1974-5. There is some evidence for both charges; that for the second is better documented than that for the first. In 1975, Sir Peter Carey, Second Permanent Secretary at

Industry, took the very rare step of writing an 'accounting officer's minute' dissociating himself from his minister's decision to continue supporting a loss-making workers' manufacturing co-operative — and somebody leaked this titbit to the Press. The Permanent Secretary, Sir Antony Part, later told a TV interviewer that he used to 'first of all try and persuade him (Benn) that he was wrong and if I thought I wasn't getting anywhere I'd try something a bit harder and we'd really start hitting each other verbally across the table'. Benn's PPS[3] complained that the Department of Trade (and he probably intended to include Industry) 'contains civil servants who are steeped in 19th century Board of Trade attitudes', namely passionate devotion to free trade.[4] (Sedgemore 1980, pp. 138-9, 232; Kellner and Crowther-Hunt 1980, pp. 179-80).

What does all this add up to? There will never be an answer to satisfy both sides. Those who want to believe that civil servants are impartial public servants will argue that the Department of Industry did nothing improper, and that everybody in the game knew that the rest of the Cabinet supported Carey and not Benn. Those who want to believe that bureaucrats subvert the people's will (or at any rate the government's) will contend that stories like these are typical. The author's judgment, but it can only be a judgment, is that stories like these are not typical, and that both extreme views underestimate the subtlety and sophistication of the Civil Service mind. Of course civil servants have strong views. Of course there is often a 'departmental view' (though critics should remember that different departments have contradictory views). But faced with a determined government, civil servants will cheerfully buckle down to tackle problems they privately think are insoluble or at any rate not soluble in the way the government proposes. It is the same sort of mental challenge as *The Times* crossword. This attitude emerged clearly over the Labour government's Scottish and Welsh devolution proposals from 1976 to 1979. First of all, there were conflicting departmental views: the Scottish and Welsh Offices were unsurprisingly in favour of further devolution to themselves, while the Cabinet Office and the Department of Industry were against. The antis won the main Whitehall battles. The Department of Industry kept control of most selective assistance to industry, and thus ensured that the putative Scottish Assembly would not control the one sort of public spending it most wanted to. The Cabinet Office intervened to prevent the Scottish Office from writing the

Scottish constitution, and kept control of it under a doggedly anti-devolutionist Permanent Secretary, Sir John Garlick.

Thus far, the evidence may seem to back the 'bureaucrats usurp power' hypothesis. But the story is really more complicated. In the first place, most of the government were, and the bureaucrats knew that they were, at root opposed to devolution — they were forced into it in order to be seen to give the people of Scotland what they wanted (and to get in return enough Labour votes to win the next Election). The Department of Industry's attitude to Scotland was quite consistent with its attitude to the North of England. It was flatly opposed to any devolution of its powers to either area, for reasons which seemed good to Ministers when applied to the North of England. As it turned out, devolution was also massively unpopular with the electorate of the United Kingdom; however, it is to the credit of the bureaucrats that they never used that as an argument for obstruction, since in a democracy it must be entirely and wholly for elected politicians to take the consequences of enacting unpopular policies. And when Ministers indicated what they wanted to be done, the civil servants buckled down to conducting what one of them cheerfully called a 'damage control operation'. The Government was committed to an unworkable policy; the challenge to the best brains in the country was to make it as nearly workable as possible. It was a challenge to which they rose with some relish. Both extreme views are wrong. Civil servants are not Olympian administrators detachedly choosing 'the best' policy; neither are they systematic subverters of the will of the elected representatives of the people.[5]

Internal affairs

Niskanen's thesis is primarily about bureaucrats' *procedures*, not their *policies*. Grocers do not mind whether they sell muesli or cornflakes, so long as they make a profit. They would worry about the contents of the packets they sold only if one sort of packet brought them consistently less surplus than another. If the analogy is sound, civil servants will care much less which policies they apply to governing Britain than which policies they apply to the government of the Civil Service. A Deputy Secretary at the Civil Service Department recently drew the distinction quite explicitly:

We must, I think, distinguish energy from commitment. It is absolutely necessary to pursue today's policy with energy; it is almost equally necessary, in order to survive, to withhold from it the last ounce of commitment. At the same time, however, I believe that it *is* possible to care, and to care passionately, to throw in the last ounce of commitment, for the idea of service itself; and to invest that commitment in our particular institution, the Civil Service itself, with all its manifest imperfections. (Quoted in Kellner and Crowther-Hunt 1980, p. 286.)

'The idea of service itself'. The phrase can be interpreted in a friendly way: if politicians and the public will an end, they must will the means. Too often a feeling gets abroad that 'the Government should do something about' (say) regulating used-car sales, to be followed by indignation at the discovery that regulation entails bureaucrats. In these circumstances, it is unfair to blame the bureaucrats. However, it is possible to be less charitable about the bureaucrats' self-defence. In particular, people who say they are committed to 'the idea of service itself' may be really saying that they are committed to bureaucratic as opposed to non-bureaucratic ways of doing things. If the alternatives are traditionalism or charisma or George Washington Plunkitt, perhaps they are right; if one of them is laissez-faire (an option Weber did not consider) it is less clear. In any case, it should be for politicians and not bureaucrats to decide. The decision whether to enforce a particular public policy by bureaucratic or non-bureaucratic means is itself a political, not a bureaucratic matter; but politicians may be forced to rely on bureaucrats' advice on whether and how to dismantle bureaucracy. Perhaps this helps to explain the puzzling case of pollution externalities. Pollution is a case of market failure. The unfettered market will not stop factories from pouring effluent into streams or Los Angeles motorists from poisoning their own atmosphere. Government must intervene, but as we noted in Chapter 5, it typically intervenes with bureaucratic regulations rather than taxes on those who pollute or subsidies to them for stopping their pollution — even though most economists believe that tax or subsidy solutions are more efficient than regulatory ones.[6] One reason for all this may be that bureaucrats are naturally likelier to see the advantages of bureaucratic solutions, and the disadvantages of market ones, than the converse.

This hypothesis has never been properly tested. One thing that is crystal clear, however, is that bureaucrats do obstruct the efforts of governments, such as the Thatcher administration of 1979, which have a policy of cutting down on bureaucracy *per se*. Soon after taking office, the Thatcher government instructed each civil service department to prepare schemes for 10, 15 and 20 per cent cuts in staff costs. Departments were evasive, except for the Ministry of Defence, which flatly refused to supply the schemes on the ground that they would be incompatible with the Government's manifesto commitment to increase defence expenditure. Although the commitment was actually one to better defence, not more civil servants, the Department got away with it, to begin with, although it was later brought to heel. Other departments insisted that costs could be cut only by cutting services to the public, and proposed changes (closing national museums on Sundays) that they knew perfectly well would provoke massive and articulate public protests. No doubt they were often correct in their claim that it was impossible to cut down costs without cutting services; but without erecting another bureaucracy to check the first one the Government could not tell when that claim was genuine and when it was bogus.

AMERICAN COMPARISONS

Americans have looked at bureaucracy carefully in theoretical work and much less in empirical work, unlike Britain where the reverse is true. There is no study of American bureaucracy to match the comprehensive ones on Britain drawn on in the last section. However, something must be said about the differences between the two countries' bureaucracies. The first, and biggest, difference is that there is no unified 'Civil Service' in the United States. The pyramid is cut off at the top. The senior posts in each department are political appointments, and every time there is a change of Administration, the senior officials appointed by the outgoing President can expect to have to pack their bags and make way for the new President's nominees. A professional administrator therefore will normally stay in one department, and will not get to the top of that — in contrast to the British mandarin going from one spending department to the Treasury to another spending department. As the career prospects are less good, so is the calibre of graduate recruits. In the USA, the best and the brightest do *not* apply for jobs in the federal (or any other) civil service.

Secondly, bureaux have less control over their own budgets than in Britain. The separation of powers means that the legislature — Congress — has some control over bureaux' budgets or 'appropriations'. Bureaucrats are serving two masters — the legislature and the executive. If a House Committee wants to appropriate money for one purpose and the Cabinet member at the head of the bureau wants to use it for another, bureaucrats are in a dilemma that has no British equivalent.

In the third place, there is far more open government than in Britain. Whereas in Britain it is an offence under the Official Secrets Acts to disclose the existence, let alone the membership, of Cabinet committees, in the United States the First Amendment and the Freedom of Information Act put the onus of proof on the body wishing information to remain secret. It is increasingly common for investigators into alleged skulduggery in Britain to get their information in the US under US law — for instance, the evidence relating to the British intelligence services' knowledge of Sir Anthony Blunt's spying activities was revealed in this way.

Fourth, the looser structure of government leads to more competition between bureaux. The Army Corps of Engineers and the Tennessee Valley Authority both build dams; the FBI and the CIA both root out 'subversives'. The most important aspect of this is that there is a relatively large bureau, responsible to the legislature, which reports on the performance of other bureaux — the General Accounting Office. (There is also one responsible to the executive in the Office of Management and Budget. Their rough British equivalents are the Exchequer and Audit Department and the Treasury respectively).

What differences in the position of bureaucrats arise from these four factors? From the first it follows that bureaux are under much closer political control than in Britain and it is therefore unlikely that a bureau would pursue a 'departmental policy' unrelated to the wishes of the executive (the main exception is the FBI under J. Edgar Hoover which paid no respect to any body, institution or Constitution). The first two factors also lead to a much more fragmented bureaucracy: if there is less political tension *within* departments than in Britain there is more *between* them. As there is no unified Civil Service, there is no 'Permanent Secretaries' network', (nor Private Secretaries', nor Ministers' drivers') on which departments can find out about each other.

The third and fourth differences open up wider gulfs between American and British practice. The British ruling class inhabits a village called Whitehall, where behind the stockade of the Official Secrets Act it practises (among consenting adults, of course) the private government of public money (Heclo and Wildavsky 1974). That is what makes it so hard to tell whether the changes of bureaucratic interference in government policy have any substance or not. But one recent development is noteworthy: aggressive leaking. When one player in the village game is outraged by what he considers flagrant breaches of the rules by the others, he tells somebody outside the village. The most striking thing about Sir Peter Carey's accounting officer's minute on Mr Benn and the Kirkby co-operative was not that he wrote it, but that somebody leaked it. And a quantum leap in hole size came with the verbatim leak of an entire Cabinet paper to an education weekly in 1981, presumably by a dissident mandarin who wished to make the policy it advocated unworkable by revealing the secret reasons for it.[7] Politicians are in no position to demand an end to aggressive leaking, since they do it even more. The organised hypocrisy of blanket secrecy tempered by self-interested leaking suits both parties; but as it suits politicians even more (on balance, they have more to hide) it is unlikely to change.[8]

Thus non-villagers get haphazard glimpses, but no more, of what goes on inside the stockade. One glimpse revealed the weakness of the bureau that is supposed to check other bureaux — the Exchequer and Audit Department. Its head, the Comptroller and Auditor-General, is supposed to be a servant of the legislature, not the executive — he reports to the Public Accounts Committee of the House of Commons, not to any minister or department. In 1975, members of the PAC became interested in reports that substantial savings in the cost of maintaining public buildings had been made in one part of the country but not copied in others. The accounting officer of the relevant department explained the discrepancy by saying that the Army had moved out of the region in question. This was untrue. But its untruth was not uncovered by the C & AG — 'I should not expect, indeed I should not permit, my staff to spend time checking all details of an Accounting Officer's evidence', he said (quoted in Chapman 1979, p. 270). Not until fourteen months after the press, aided by the then-retired civil servant who had made the initial savings, had discovered that the accounting officer had misled the committee did he admit it (for full details and supporting documents see Chapman 1979, chs. 8 and 22 and Appendices 1, 2, 8 and 9).

Compared to the American General Accounting Office (GAO), the Exchequer and Audit Department (EAD) has two striking weaknesses. First, it is the only British bureau to be staffed by lower-calibre officers than its American equivalent. In 1975 the GAO had 3,509 graduate professional staff. In 1969 the EAD had ten graduates; by 1979 that had risen to 185 (figures from Garrett 1980, p. 176). A high proportion of its work still consists of checking for fraud and pilfering, and, as we have seen, it has neither the staff nor the skills (nor, it seems, the will) to check whether other bureaux are managing their resources efficiently, still less whether their programmes are achieving their stated aims. Secondly, it is doubtful how much the EAD is genuinely independent of the rest of the bureaucracy. Its staff are civil servants, on the same pay and conditions as those in ordinary departments, and Comptrollers and Auditors-General are often recruited from the Treasury: the present CAG called his department 'an important instrument of the Treasury' and denied that he was accountable solely, or indeed at all, to the PAC (Garrett 1980, pp. 177-180). He believed that spending departments should review their own efficiency, which should not be a job for the EAD. Thus if the public-choice theorists' suspicion that bureau chiefs tend to aggrandise their bureaux is well-founded (and there is evidence, though it falls short of proof), the British audit arrangements do not look like much of an obstacle.

CONCLUSION

The evidence of this chapter points towards qualified acceptance of the view that bureaucrats are important intermediaries with objectives that do not wholly coincide with those of the politicians whose policies they are paid to put into effect. Qualified; the case that they have unified views on *policy* is not proven, but the case that they have, and exercise, a vested interest in bureaucracy itself looks stronger. This must be balanced against an opposite vested

interest of politicians which we have not yet discussed. Given that
the public does not like bureaucrats, and does not like paying taxes,
one might expect a party which promises to cut both to do well in
elections. Indeed, in both Britain and America 'cutting the
bureaucracy' has recently become a more salient 'valence issue', in
the terminology of Chapter 2. It is easier to promise than to do. No
doubt it is partly the result of politicians' exploiting the electorate's
failure to see that if you want non-market controls you must also
pay for bureaucrats to enforce them. Nevertheless politicians with
an eye on the median voter will compete in their claims to be the
best at cutting 'bureaucracy' and 'waste'. Voters are bound to judge
these claims by results. Unless one believes, fatalistically, that
Sir Humphrey will always and everywhere get the better of Jim
Hacker, the pressure of bureaucrats to aggrandise bureau size — or
whatever else they are suspected of trying to aggrandise — will be
countered by pressure from politicians to cut them down. It would
probably be a mistake to predict total victory for either side. If
natural selection works in politics, the fittest race of politicians —
those most able to get themselves re-elected — should survive.

Part III

Politicians

Like party activists, democratic politicians are sometimes hard to fathom. It is easy to understand why Hitler or Stalin or the average South American general wanted power: if you take pleasure in amassing millions of dollars or killing millions of people, it pays to become a politician in a non-democratic regime. But in a democracy, power and wealth are elusive. Even if you lay hands on them, you may abruptly and totally lose your grip after the next election. If you really want power, you would do better as a bureaucrat; if you really want wealth, be a rock star or a property developer, not a politician.

The problem 'why does anybody become a politician?' resembles that of why anybody becomes a party activist, which was tackled in Chapter 6. Therefore the structure of the last two chapters parallels that of Chapter 6. In Chapter 8 we look at various 'entrepreneurial' explanations and in Chapter 9 at 'expressivist' ones.

8

Entrepreneurs

Harold Wilson: And why do I stress the importance of a strong Navy? . . .
Heckler: Because you're in Chatham.

Incident during General Election campaign, 1966

NON-IDEOLOGICAL ENTREPRENEURS

Until Lewis Namier's great work *The Structure of Politics at the Accession of George III* (1957; first published 1929), British historians had usually described eighteenth-century high politics in terms of principle and party. People were Whigs if they supported the constitutional settlement of 1689 and Tories if they were alarmed by the erosion of the position of the Anglican church. Namier went to the opposite extreme, and tried to show that ideology played no part at all in people's decisions to become politicians. He analysed the career of every MP elected to the House of Commons in the early 1760s, and classed them into many categories, all aggressively free from any ideological connection. He was aided by the delightfully frank letters which seat-hunters sent to the biggest patron of all, the Duke of Newcastle. Let some of them speak for themselves.
There was the social climber:

> I have never troubled your Grace for any great, much less, for any lucrative employment . . . for my fortune is sufficient for me, in any station of life, but my whole ambition centers in the hopes of a peerage for my family.
>
> (Sir John Rushout, MP, to Newcastle, 24 January 1756)

There was the naval officer who wanted promotion. Newcastle asked the great admiral Anson for promotion for an MP who wanted to become a commander, and got a forthright and pained reply:

> The King expects that I should keep up his interest in boroughs; I can't do it without I have the assistance of the several branches of the Government.
>
> (Newcastle to Anson, 15 June 1759)

> I must now beg your Grace will seriously consider what must be the condition of your Fleet if these borrough recommendations, which must be frequent are to be complyed with ... captains of that cast ... [have] done more mischeif to the publick (which I know is the most favorite point with you) than the loss of a vote in the House of Commons.
>
> (Anson to Newcastle, 15 June 1759)

There were the tradesmen:

> As the correspondence of the shop is very great, having the draughts of the Bristol Bank, the very postage of their letters would amount to near £800 pr. ann., and it is otherwise thought to be of great service to the house to have one of the partners in Parliament.
>
> (James West, MP, to Newcastle, 31 January 1764)

And there were a few desperate paupers:

> Your Grace knows my present situation well, which if it could be settled upon the Irish Establishment would fix me yours for ever.
>> (Thomas Medlycott, MP, to Newcastle, 31 December 1755)
> [To] Mr Fairfax starving — £500.
>> (Entries in Newcastle's accounts for 13 November, 24 November, 8 December and 9 December 1761. Robert Fairfax was MP for Kent).
>> (Quotations from Namier 1957, pp. 13, 33, 34, 57-8, 407, 415).

Are politicians really as unideological as that? Namier exaggerated, because it was part of his ideology to deny ideology any role in politics; but it was easy to make his case, because the records of Newcastle's slush funds are more accessible than, say, Richard Nixon's. Perhaps the 1760s were not a particularly corrupt time, but only a time when the corrupters kept meticulous accounts. Every era has its Plunkitts, its Boss Crokers, and its Advertisers, who were fully dealt with in Chapter 6. Some recent writers, however, have suggested a more subtle form of entrepreneurship (Frohlich *et al.* 1971, 1978; but cf. Laver 1980). They start, once again, with the public goods paradox. Nobody has an individual incentive to contribute to the production of national defence or clean air even though everyone wants them. Why not, then, introduce a public goods entrepreneur, to be called a 'politician', who will provide public goods in return for a fee? So long as the fee is less than the people's gain from having the public good, everybody has made something from the deal. A baker provides a private good (bread) that people want, and makes a surplus; a politician provides public goods in return for his fee. Some bakers are interested in baking for its own sake, but not all are. You might become a baker without having the smallest interest in bread, but only in making profits. No doubt your bread is not as nice as a craftsman's, but people are prepared to buy it — if they weren't, you wouldn't remain a baker for very long. Likewise, while many politicians are interested in the policies they promote, not all need be. Like Downs, Frohlich *et al.* assume that politicians' only interests lie in their re-election.

How do they finance their activities? Not, on the whole, by voluntary contributions from those who want the public good. By definition, citizens will not voluntarily pay for the good itself. There is therefore no logical reason why they should pay a politician who says he will provide it. They will not pay him beforehand, because he might walk off with the money; and they will not pay him after he has provided it either, because it is now there and he cannot exclude anybody from enjoying it without paying. Voluntary contributions apart, there are some picturesque possibilities, such as extortion (Laver 1980, p. 206), but the realistic options boil down to two: taxation, and financing by suppliers of the factors of production.

An entrepreneur who can levy taxes is in the enviable position of being free to write his own pay cheque after providing the public goods. If this power is boundless, then the difficulty of explaining why people want to be politicians vanishes. Who would not covet a job where he could freely decide how much to pay himself? The problem shifts from 'why would anybody want to do this?' to 'why would anybody ever be prepared to set this monster up in business?' Hobbes's Leviathan is just such an entrepreneur. People in the state of nature see that they need someone to provide the public goods of law and order, enforcing contracts and so on; but if, as Hobbes proposes, they give him boundless powers to punish anti-social behaviour, there is nothing to stop him behaving anti-socially himself, for instance by appropriating everybody's income in taxation and giving them nothing in return (see, e.g. McLean 1981). One school of economists has therefore argued that the only 'principle of just taxation' is a unanimity rule — no politician may impose a tax unless everybody who would have to pay it agrees in advance to it (Wicksell 1958; Mueller 1979 ch. 14). Unfortunately, this just opens up another public goods paradox[1], and they recede away into the distance like rooms in an enormous hall of mirrors.

But this approach is too pessimistic, because it does not allow for competition among entrepreneurs. In a democracy, there is always another set of entrepreneurs waiting in the wings with the claim that, if elected, they would provide the same public goods in return for a lower rate of taxation. And in Britain (though not the USA) the issue of how much politicians pay themselves is embarrassingly conspicuous. MPs are actually extremely bad at writing generous cheques to themselves. They know that a storm of protest will arise each time they propose raising their own salaries, and in consequence their pay, always low, has probably declined in real terms in recent years. Government ministers are not only paid less than pop stars and property developers; they pay themselves less than those they directly supervise, such as senior civil servants and chairmen of nationalised industries. Elected public office, both national and local, is seriously underpaid in Britain, but even so many MPs and local councillors rather ostentatiously tell their voters that they are not drawing their salaries. Because they are not merely entrepreneurs, but competitive entrepreneurs, they tend to reduce their profit margins.

Their other main source of income comes from suppliers of the factors of production — land, labour and capital — in the hope of profitable contracts. If a politician is to provide public goods, he must use somebody's capital and somebody's labour to produce them. Controllers of labour (such as trade unions) and capital (such as manufacturing companies) therefore have an interest in providing funds to help politicians get elected. They do so in both Britain and the USA, but in very different ways reflecting enormously different legal and political traditions.

CAMPAIGN FINANCE IN BRITAIN AND THE USA

Britain

Britain has the cheapest politics of any democracy, thanks to that most effective of Victorian political reforms, the Corrupt and Illegal Practices Act of 1883. Before 1883, campaigning was very expensive. Candidates spent freely on drinks, conveyances, and straightforward bribes. The Ballot Act of 1872 was expected to end all this by providing for the secret ballot but, if anything, it had the opposite effect: voters could now cheerfully take bribes from both sides, with neither being able to prove that they had got any return from their investment. The General Election of 1880 was one of the most corrupt in British history. In Macclesfield, where a subsequent inquiry accused 2,872 named people of corruption, two entrepreneurs at a copper works offered their workmates' votes to the Conservatives at 10/- (50p) each, with a commission of £2.10.0 (£2.50) for themselves. They then went round to the Liberals, who matched the Conservatives' price in return for a promise that the workers would vote as they pleased. In Oxford, at a by-election soon after, a Tory secret slush-fund of £3,000 was revealed by accident when an academic absent-mindedly dropped a letter about it in the High Street. The Liberals spent £3,275 and the Conservatives £3,611 on the campaign. In 1981 prices, that represents approximately £185,000 altogether. There were just over 5,000 electors in Oxford at the time, so the total expenditure per elector was nearly £1.38 at 1880 prices or £37 in present-day terms (O'Leary 1962, pp. 141-2 (Macclesfield); 146-7 (Oxford)).

It is very rare for anything to be swept away as abruptly and completely as this was. The 1883 Act laid down stringent maxima, such that no candidate would be allowed to spend much over £700 (O'Leary 1962, pp. 161, 175). Since 1883, the expenditure limits have become many times more stringent still in real terms. They were not raised when the electorate was enlarged in 1918 and 1928 — which cut permitted expenditure per voter by three-quarters or so. And they have never risen in line with inflation, whereas the cost of things that candidates buy has done. So British politicians have failed not only to pay themselves but even to let other people pay them. In 1979, the average permitted maximum expenditure per candidate was £3,050 in boroughs and £2,725 in county constituencies; Conservative candidates on average spent 79 per cent of their maxima and Labour candidates 72 per cent (Butler and Kavanagh 1980, pp. 315-6). It was thus illegal for a candidate to spend more than 4½ pence per elector in the 1979 General Election.

Candidates have access to some free facilities: for instance, one mailshot to each household in the constituency, and the use of public buildings for meetings; and the television companies must give parties free air time for their political broadcasts. But this makes little difference to the picture of extreme stringency just painted. The 1883 Act does not cover day-to-day party expenditure, when no election is in the offing, nor central expenditure by the parties (e.g. on national advertising) at a General Election. In 1883 national party organisations were in their infancy, and hardly existed at all outside election periods, and therefore nobody thought of including them in the restrictive legislation. It might be thought, therefore, that the British, especially suppliers of the factors of production, would pour their political contributions in at these points. So they do; but extremely stingily. Table 8.1 gives the only recent estimates of constituency (but not ward) and central party income for a non-General Election year.

TABLE 8.1

BRITISH POLITICAL PARTIES: ESTIMATED INCOME 1975

	Central £	Constituency £	Total £
Conservative	1,790,000	4,500,000	6,290,000
Labour	1,200,000	1,750,000	2,950,000
Liberal	113,000	750,000	863,000
Scottish and Welsh Nationalist	145,000	160,000	305,000

Source: Houghton (1976), ch. 6

In a General Election year, these figures go up, but not by very much. First estimates suggest that the major parties raised and spent about £1 million each in the 1979 General Election campaign (Butler and Kavanagh 1980, pp. 57, 71, 319). Most of this money does indeed come from producer-group organisations representing labour or capital. About 90 per cent of Labour's central income comes from trade unions (more than for any other major democratic socialist party); and well over half of the Conservatives' central income is from company contributions. This shows not that producer groups contribute exceptionally heavily to British party finance but that hardly anybody else contributes at all. Even producer-group contributions are less than in many other democracies.

Furthermore, many of them are involuntary. If a company decides to contribute funds to a political organisation, there is no way in which its shareholders can opt out if they disagree. And trade unions operate a 'contracting out' rule: that is, their members are deemed to wish to contribute to the political fund unless they expressly deny that they do. Inertia is the Labour Party's staunchest recruiting sergeant, closely followed by ignorance. More trade unionists are actually 'members' of the Labour Party than voted for it in 1974 or 1979.

Since both voluntary contributions and grants from producer groups have declined, and quite seriously, in recent years, some British politicians have sought out a new sort of taxation to finance themselves directly in the form of state aid to political parties. In 1975 the Labour government allocated money for research facilities for opposition parties in Parliament, and appointed an official committee under a former Labour minister, Lord Houghton, to look at ways of giving public money to political parties in the country. The Houghton Committee could not produce an agreed report. But its majority argued that parties were essential to democracy and the normal 'means whereby members of the general public are able to participate in the formulation of policies' (Houghton 1976, para 3.4). It proposed that each party should be eligible for an annual grant of 5p. per vote received at the previous general election, and that election expenses up to half the legal maximum should be refunded to candidates in national and local elections who got over one-eighth of the votes cast.

The parties which gave evidence to Houghton were by no means all in favour of state aid. The Labour Party and the English and

Welsh Liberals were in favour; the Conservatives, the Scottish Liberals and the Communists were among those opposed. Their reasons ranged from the need to keep parties independent of 'the power of the state and state bureaucracy' (Conservative) to the danger of parties becoming less responsive to their members (Communist). Furthermore, the Houghton majority did not make their case very well. They did not specify what party functions were essential to democracy, and therefore could not prove that the parties had become too poor to carry them out. They ignored the best arguments for state aid (e.g. that without it the parties of the rich may speak louder than the parties of the poor, or the free-rider argument that the existence of parties in a democracy is a public good which voluntary contributions will therefore always under-finance). Four members of the committee submitted a trenchant minority report which cuttingly exposed many of the weaknesses of the main report (though some of their own arguments were also weak). The report had a chilly reception. *The Times,* for instance, demanded scornfully: 'Send Them Empty-handed Away', and noted that the report had been 'greeted with such opposition from almost every point of the political compass' that it would be impossible to enact.[2] They were right; and a more recent unofficial report (Hansard Society 1981) is unlikely to gain any more widespread support.

America

Politicians in Britain have thus signally failed to finance even their re-election, let alone their running expenses, from taxation or producer-group contributions. Whatever they are, they are not non-ideological entrepreneurs. The position in the USA is rather different. The United States never had a Corrupt and Illegal Practices Act (anything of the sort would probably have been ruled unconstitutional), so that there has been nothing to stop election expenditure from touching the dizzy heights it reached in Britain in 1880. The all-comers' individual record to date belongs to John D. Rockefeller IV, the Democratic governor of West Virginia. As the saying went in 1980, 'The good news is that you can still buy West Virginia. The bad news is, boy, is it expensive'. In 1980 Rockefeller was re-elected after spending about $11.75 million on his campaign — about $30 per vote he received.[3]

Some Americans have long been alarmed that the costs of campaigning may exclude the poor, or at least those without rich friends. The Federal Election Campaign Act 1971 (amended in 1974 and 1976) tried to help the poor and curb the rich. After Watergate, whose 'dirty tricks' in 1972 were largely done and financed by CREEP (the Committee to Re-elect the President), it had widespread support. But observers warned (Ranney 1979), and the 1980 elections proved, that it would spectacularly fail to achieve what the reformers wanted.

The main reforms were as follows. No individual could pay more than $1,000 to any one candidate, and no organisation over $5,000. A candidate for a presidential nomination who could raise at least $5,000 in small individual contributions was eligible for matching Federal assistance up to a limit of $5 million; but he could not then spend over $10 million in all. Likewise a duly nominated candidate could not spend over $20 million in the general election if he accepted Federal funds. All Presidential aspirants accepted Federal money in 1976, and all except John Connally did in 1980.

This legislation failed in 1980 for a number of reasons. It could not, even if successful, have brought campaign expenditure down to British levels — for instance it covered only campaigns for federal office, and the limits it set seem absurdly high to British eyes (just as Americans find the British limits incomprehensibly low). We might measure the dimensions of its failure in 1980, and then try to assess the reasons.

The Presidential candidates were held to $29.4 million each, and $4.6 million more to be spent by their national party organisations on their direct behalf. But first estimates suggested that the Carter and Reagan campaigns would cost over $100 million between them because of local and state party spending for them and, especially, of independent groups campaigning for the candidates without going through the party organisations. In 1980 most of these groups were for Reagan.[4]

But Presidential expenditure is only the tip of the iceberg. Senate, House and gubernatorial races also broke all spending records. By 15 October 1980, Representative Robert K. Dornan (R.- Calif.) had spent nearly $1.5 million to defend his House seat. And when one candidate splashed money around, his opponents did so as well if they could afford to: Dornan's Democratic opponent spent $401,343, which was only the twenty-third highest sum spent by a candidate for the House in 1980.[5]

Some of the biggest spenders were not parties or candidates' organisations but Political Action Committees (PACs). Some cynics called the 1980 campaign the Pacs Americana. As individuals could spend only $1,000 each on a candidate but organisations could spend $5,000, there was an obvious incentive to found organisations to send (officially unsolicited) money to candidates. All sorts of groups — producer, consumer, and altruistic — set up PACs in order to pump millions of dollars into the Senate and House races of candidates who supported them. There was no upper limit on either the number of candidates a PAC could support or the number of PACs which could support one candidate.

The *Washington Post* studied the campaign finances of Congressmen who sat on committees with massive spending powers, especially the House Ways and Means Committee and the Senate Finance Committee. In 1980 all except four of the 40 members of these committees who were up for re-election got substantial funds from PACs, to the sum of $3 million, which represented 34 per cent of their election receipts. (The other four were offered PAC money but refused it). From the American Medical Association ($66,400) to the Carpenters and Joiners union ($30,050) the top ten PACs were all producer groups — labour, management or farming.[6] Although the most conspicuous and most talked-about PACs were right-wing altruistic ones which channelled money to help defeat legislators whose views on abortion, creationism or the Panama Canal treaties they disliked, the biggest-spending PACs seem to have been not these, but (as the theory of Chapter 5 would lead us to expect) the producer group ones. Moreover, some of these PACs financed challengers as well as incumbents — they wanted their group's interests to be advanced whoever won the election. And it was not just a matter of election-time financing. House members face an election every two years, and therefore must spend a lot of their time and money electioneering. But their favourite PACs look after them well, with more or less continuous financing. An American politician, unlike a British one, might quite legally aim for a career in moneymaking, pure and simple, without ever adopting any opinions except his paymasters'. Of course, he would not start making really rich profits until he had secured a place on a high-spending congressional committee, but he should be able to calculate how much he could afford to invest in getting on to one in order to be sure of an adequate return.

Two legislators, both Democrats, provide interesting rival perspectives on this. Charles A. Vanik of Ohio declared that he would not stand again after thirteen terms in the House. He refused to raise large sums of campaign money and criticised others for doing so. It had, he claimed, produced a Congress with 'little stability or courage . . . I feel every contribution carries some sort of lien which is an encumbrance on the legislative process. Contributions are rewarded by legislative policy. This is bought and sold'[7]. Larry McDonald of Georgia took a different view. He was a close friend of the Bunker Hunt brothers who tried to corner the silver market in 1979 and 1980. Rep. McDonald introduced and fought for a bill committing the Federal administration to buying $500 millions' worth of silver for the Defense Department's stockpile of strategic metals. 'Silver will be the first of the strategic metals the world will run out of', he claimed: a view not shared by the Defense Department. Even though the bill failed, it produced a speculative rise in the price of silver, which the Hunts had been secretly buying before it was introduced. In 1976 five members of the Hunt family contributed the legal maximum of $1,000 each to Rep. McDonald's election funds; in 1978 three members did; and in 1979 ten did. It helps to have a large family. Rep. McDonald's campaign funds actually showed a profit over this period.[8]

There are two main reasons why attempts to restrict campaign spending have failed so signally. First, it is a significant restriction of liberty to limit the amounts of money that citizens may give to causes they support. And in the USA, some liberties are entrenched, so that laws purporting to override them can be ruled unconstitutional. This happened to several sections of the Federal Election Campaign Act, which were held to violate the 'freedom of speech and the press' section of the First Amendment.[9] The Constitution sometimes makes strange bedfellows. In an allied case in October 1980, the Internal Revenue Service reversed an earlier ruling that a charity would lose its tax-exempt status if it published 'score-cards' rating legislators for their stands on issues the charity was interested in. The score-card technique — to its enemies the 'hit-list' — is mostly a weapon of the far right, and it was used extensively in 1980 by the fundamentalist Christian PACs to decide which legislators to oppose; but it was defended as a First Amendment right by the American Civil Liberties Union, which called the IRS's climbdown 'a major victory for free speech'.[10]

The second reason is the weakness of parties and the division of responsibility for public spending between the executive and the legislature. Congressmen are worth lobbying because the Congress takes decisions, unlike the British Parliament. In Britain, in so far as any group finances anybody, the producer groups finance *parties* in the hope that one they favour will form the government and act in their interests; in the USA they finance *individuals*. The government cannot satisfy all the groups all the time; in a party system this is more obvious than in a non-party one, and it may deter pressure groups from trying to buy support for their policies. Britain in the 1760s and the 1880s, and the USA now, all had weak party systems in which alliances were based on unpredictable coalitions of individual entrepreneurs. Reformers, on the whole, deplore this situation. So they try to put the politics into politics and take the corruption (as they see it) out. It is a pity that American reformers have such an infallible knack for doing the wrong thing. For FECA has had the same effect as the Progressive constitutional reforms of the turn of the century. It has made parties even weaker (because Federal money goes to candidates, not parties, and because of the unforeseen but apparently irresistible rise of the PACs), and therefore made it even harder to achieve the reformers' objectives. The comparison makes the 1883 Corrupt and Illegal Practices Act seem even more remarkable in retrospect.

IDEOLOGICAL ENTREPRENEURS

Non-ideological entrepreneurship can thus account for some politicians (Thomas Medlycott, Larry McDonald), but not very many. In Britain, campaign costs are low, so that it would be cheap for producer-groups to pay not only for politicians' election but for their upkeep. However, they are very stingy and hardly pay for their election. In the USA, producer groups are very much more generous. But almost all their generosity is swallowed up in campaign costs. We have now got some explanation of how and why politicians can raise that sort of money from other people, but not of why they should want to spend their own (like Rockefeller) or why they want to be in the legislature at all. The next step is to look at entrepreneurs with opinions of their own.

For J. Q. Wilson, who has done most to develop the concept, (Wilson 1974, 1980) a policy entrepreneur is somebody who either mobilises, or persuades government that he can mobilise, a majority for a policy that otherwise might not get enacted. It is not enough for a project to have majority support. If the many who are for it are not prepared to put resources into the effort of lobbying for it, whereas the few who are against are prepared to lobby because they have something substantial to lose, the project will not get through. We have seen that this is likely in cases where producers have an interest on the opposite side to consumers'. So the wonder is not that pro-consumer legislation is imperfect and inefficient but that it exists at all. Wilson actually defines as 'entrepreneurial politics' the cases where most people expect that the costs of a policy will be concentrated on relatively few and the benefits will be spread more widely (Wilson 1980, pp. 419, 434-7). That is the purest case; but the term can be used more broadly. Here are one American and two British cases to show the range of styles of ideological entrepreneurship.

The career of Ralph Nader is too well known to require summarising here. He leapt to fame in the 1960s after General Motors had made a crude attempt to blacken his character after he had denounced their cars as unsafe. (If they had employed a statistician instead of a private detective, history might have been different.) The image of the little man battling against faceless big money is so potent in US political folklore that Nader gained enormous popular support. He was not a member of any branch of the government, nor interested in becoming one; indeed, he attacked his own ex-aides for taking executive jobs. But you can be an entrepreneur without being a legislator; it is enough to be able to persuade legislators that they will gain from adopting your policy, or lose from not adopting it, or both. Tougher auto safety and emission control regulations seemed to transfer costs from consumers, especially victims of accidents and pollution, to producers.[11] So how were they passed? Because Nader was able to persuade legislators that there were votes in it. Senators Ribicoff and Magnusson, who sponsored Nader's auto safety bill, were politicians looking for an issue; Nader was an issue-campaigner looking for a politician; a deal profitable to both was struck (Wilson 1980, p. 435). The Senators, in this case, were non-ideological entrepreneurs searching for a vote-winning issue; Nader was an ideological entrepreneur acting as a middle-man between voters who wanted a policy and politicians who were prepared to provide it.

My two British examples each involve a key Act of Parliament that has shaped modern Britain (the Trade Disputes Act 1906 and the National Insurance Act 1946) and its key entrepreneur — the now-forgotten David Shackleton and the well-remembered William Beveridge, respectively.

In 1900, the British courts ruled that the railway union was liable to pay the Taff Vale railway company damages to compensate it for its loss of income during a strike. If that judgment was not reversed, trade unions would risk bankruptcy every time any of their members struck. Naturally, the Trades Union Congress wanted to get Taff Vale reversed and they looked to David Shackleton, one of the first independent Labour MPs, to help them. In principle there were two legislative ways of reversing Taff Vale, a narrow way and a broad way. Unions must be given immunity from civil actions for conspiracy to do what would not be actionable if done by an individual; and they should not be liable for damages after they had called official strikes in pursuance of a trade dispute. That was the narrow view, which many Liberals and some Conservatives, as well as the handful of Labour MPs, could support. The broad strategy removed the last qualification: *any* action, official or not, authorised or not, was to be immune so long as it was done 'in contemplation or furtherance of a trade dispute'. That was much too radical for almost every Liberal and Conservative — and yet it was pushed through a House of Commons in which the Liberals and the Conservatives held 457 of the 670 seats between them, and ever since has formed the highly distinctive basis of British industrial relations law. How did this come about?

In 1903 Shackleton proposed the narrow bill with Liberal support, but it was defeated by the Conservative majority. Then the TUC switched to supporting the radical bill, partly because the costs to labour of Taff Vale were turning out much higher than expected, partly because the Government appointed a Royal Commission on the matter which was stuffed with known opponents of the TUC view. Shackleton now got the left-wing Liberals to abandon the narrow bill in favour of his, and also recruited the Irish Party in return for a promise to widen the definition of 'conspiracy' in the bill in order to protect the activities of the United Irish League. The

TUC's bill was introduced in 1904 and 1905 by sympathetic Liberals, but unsurprisingly failed after its second reading both times.

Some Liberals did not like the broad bill, believing that 'trade unions should be liable for wrongful acts when they expressly authorised these wrongful acts';[12] but many happily went into the 1906 election campaign pledged to it. Shackleton and his colleagues had lobbied them intensively with warnings that they must not alienate their working-class constituents. Candidates who were not lawyers and did not know very much about the issue probably could not see that there was much at stake between the two versions of the bill; but even some of those who could had also rashly pledged in their election campaigns to support the TUC bill. In March 1906 the Liberals introduced the narrow bill. In the face of furious protests from the Labour members that this breached their election promises, the Prime Minister, Campbell-Bannerman, intervened in the middle of the debate to withdraw his own bill in favour of the Labour one, which then passed without difficulty.[13] It was perhaps the most remarkable triumph of a minor party this century.

William Beveridge was involved in shaping British social policy for 35 years. As a civil servant at the Board of Trade he had helped to lay the foundations of the Welfare State between 1908 and 1911; and his report *Social Insurance and Allied Services* of 1942 formed the basis of the modern edifice as erected in the National Insurance Act of 1946. In 1942, his technical problem was to devise a system which was nominally contributory but actually covered all the hardest cases, as no insurance-based scheme could practicably do.[14] His political problem was similar to Shackleton's: how to get legislation through a Parliament where only a minority of members supported it (the wartime coalition was dominated by the Conservatives). Beveridge was a ruthless publicist and he created and encouraged a massive wave of public opinion on his side. The Beveridge Report had one of the largest sales ever of a government report, and a shortened version was issued for discussion in every army unit until the Government decided that Beveridge's publicity had gone too far and withdrew it. Undaunted, Beveridge set up a private committee on economic policy, and the second, unofficial Beveridge Report, *Full Employment in a Free Society,* was almost as influential as the first, with which it is indeed often confused.

Beveridge's proposals were substantially different to the traditional policy of the Labour Party, which had wanted a non-contributory system, but his campaign of 1942-5 captured the Labour Party and the whole country. The massive rejection of the Conservatives in the 1945 General Election owed something (even if not so much as was once claimed) to this, and to the fact that Churchill, who was uninterested in domestic policy, gave Beveridge only a half-hearted and grudging acknowledgement in the election campaign.[15]

The protagonists of these three dramas have very little in common, but they are all ideological entrepreneurs. One was an outsider, one an opposition MP, and one an irregular bureaucrat. Each provided a public good[16] which would otherwise not have been provided, and did so because he wanted it to be provided. He was neither a non-ideological entrepreneur nor somebody who was in politics primarily for power or glory or love. The first stage of entrepreneurship is convincing legislators that there is a popular majority for your proposal, and that they stand to lose votes by opposing it. It does not matter whether your claim is true or not; it does matter that legislators should be made to believe that it is true. The next stage is implementation. A popular majority is not enough on its own to enact a policy if it needs the co-operation of producer groups. We shall look in the next section at a striking example.

HOW ENTREPRENEURS WIN VOTES AND HOW THEY
KEEP THEM

A government which could convince the voters on the eve of every election that they were getting richer and would continue to get richer might never lose. This is a fact which politicians have known for centuries and academics for a decade or two. The British Conservative governments of the 1950s and 1960s were remarkably successful at engineering a boom by fiscal changes just before an election which had to be paid for just after it (for details see Brittan 1971). No more recent British government has succeeded, partly because the British economy is too hard to control and partly because of the uncertainty of the date of the next election. American Presidents, with their fixed terms, have tried more consistently. Tufte (1980) studied the most visible of all political manipulations of voters' real wealth: cash transfers from the government to individual citizens (pensions, social security checks and so on). He found that in non-election years their cash value sloped steadily up each month to peak in December. In election years, without exception, they peaked in October or November. Nor was that all. Election day is always the first Tuesday in November, but government cheques for a month are distributed to post offices in advance, with instructions to be delivered on the third of the month. Tufte therefore predicted that in years when the first Tuesday fell on the sixth or seventh of November, the peak month for the cash value of transfers would be November, otherwise it would be October. That is exactly what the record shows.

In October 1972, over 24 million recipients of social security checks received the following message with their monthly check:

Higher Social Security Payments
Your social security payment has been increased by 20 per cent, starting with this month's check, by a new statute enacted by the Congress and signed into law by President Richard Nixon on 1 July 1972.

The President also signed into law a provision which will allow your social security benefits to increase automatically if the cost of living goes up. Automatic benefit increases will be added to your check in future years according to the conditions set out in that law.

(US Dept. of Health, Education, and Welfare circular no. (SSA) 73-10322; quoted by Tufte (1980), p. 32).

Richard Nixon is not the only president to have tried the gambit, merely the most ruthless. The art, of course, lies not in making people better off but in making them think they are better off. Real disposable income of the American people increased by exactly the same amount (3.3 per cent) in 1972 and 1976. However, election-day surveys produced the data in Table 8.2 on how people thought their financial state had changed during the year. President Nixon won re-election in 1972; President Ford failed to in 1976. As Tufte comments, 'The extremes of 1972 were special because Richard Nixon was special' (p. 63).

If you can make everybody feel better off as an election approaches and force them to pay afterwards, *and* if people have memories shorter than the interval to the next election, you might win every one. Fortunately for democracy, some people have long memories;

TABLE 8.2

REPORTED FAMILY FINANCIAL CONDITION DURING YEAR:
US NATIONAL SURVEYS

	1972 %	1976 %
Improved	36	22
Same	42	50
Deteriorated	22	28
	100	100

Source: Tufte (1980) pp. 126-7.

some voters' choices are moulded by very ancient, even inherited, memories. A more subtle ploy is to make payments from the government in highly visible forms — such as social security cheques — and to take payments back in much less easily spotted forms, such as indirect taxation or simply allowing inflation to happen. However, there are cases where politicians cannot fool all of the people even some of the time: especially matters not of economic policy, but of zero-sum conflicts in which a gain by one group represents an equal and opposite loss by another. Let us look at how some entrepreneurs have coped with this problem.

David Lloyd George was one of the most successful entrepreneurs, both at mobilising his own support and at implementing policy, in British political history. He was first elected for the by no means safe Liberal seat of Caernarvon Boroughs in 1890 as a campaigner for the values of Welsh non-conformity: restoration of the language, disestablishment of the Anglican church, land reform. By 1906 he had lost any serious interest in Welsh affairs, and for the rest of his career he pursued many causes (and led a lifestyle) that would have deeply offended his constituents if they had known about them. But he made his seat safe and kept it that way by orating with great *hwyl* to his constituents on what did concern them, as newsreel films of the 1930s show. Of course, those who did not speak Welsh (including his fellow politicians in London) had not the least idea of what he was saying.

He applied his talents to the toughest zero-sum problem of all — Ireland. By 1918, it was obvious that the objectives of the Catholic

Republicans and the Protestant Unionists in Ireland were starkly incompatible. The first wanted the whole of Ireland to be an independent sovereign state, the second wanted the whole of Ireland to remain an integral part of the UK. The partition into North and South that was emerging in an *ad hoc* way satisfied neither. (It is a pervasive and tenacious but utterly baseless myth that in creating Northern Ireland the British were giving the Protestants what they wanted). Only brilliant footwork enabled Lloyd George to sell Partition to both sides and to his own Tory colleagues, end the Anglo-Irish war of 1919-21 and conclude the Treaty of 1921. He simultaneously persuaded the Protestants that Britain would protect the territorial integrity of Northern Ireland and the Catholics that it would not. Michael Collins, one of the southern Irish negotiators, wrote immediately before signing the treaty recognising an Irish Free State without the North: 'We would save Tyrone and Fermanagh, parts of Derry, Antrim, and Down by the Boundary Commission . . . Lloyd George remarked that I myself pointed out on a previous occasion that the North would be forced economically to come in' (quoted in Pakenham 1967, p. 258). Would-be entrepreneurs should study that last sentence very carefully. Lloyd George told no lies. But the Boundary Commission went the North's way. North and South hated each other so much that neither checked with the other what Lloyd George had given them to understand.

There are more recent, if less spectacular, examples in British politics. 'Yes' campaigners in the Welsh devolution referendum of 1979 told Welsh-speakers (in Welsh) that a 'Yes' vote would protect the language and its speakers; they told non-Welsh-speakers (in English) that it would not. At least they could use the language to smooth the very problem it had created. A similar problem arose at the same time with Scottish devolution. The Labour government had to give the Scots the impression that their proposed Assembly would channel much more money into Scotland and to give Tynesiders and Liverpudlians the impression that it would not. In October 1974 the Labour Party transmitted different party political broadcasts to Scotland and to England. The Scottish ones stressed that Labour would introduce a 'parliament' in Edinburgh, which would have 'powers of taxation and revenue', and would control the Scottish Development Agency which would in turn be 'primed by North Sea oil so that the benefits of oil go to the ordinary working people of Scotland' (all quotations from Miller 1981, p. 70).

The English did not know what the Scots were being promised. When they found out, they were upset — especially in poor areas such as Tyneside and Merseyside. So the Labour government issued a soothing White Paper (Office of the Ld. Pres. of the Council 1976): it stressed that after devolution to Scotland and Wales the central government would 'retain direct control over economic management and over regional policy, industrial policy and commercial policy' and would use these powers to ensure 'that industrial investment is "steered" to the assisted areas and that resources continue to be allocated to the different countries of the United Kingdom in accordance with needs' (paras. 43, 44).

The homogeneity of the UK places tight limits on operations of this sort. It is hard for politicians to say one thing in one place and another in another because nationwide media penetrate every corner of the land. Significantly, our three examples all involve the parts of the UK which they penetrate least — Scotland, Wales and Ireland. For instance, Scotland and Wales have separate TV news bulletins, and the 'national' press circulates very few copies in Scotland. When the opposite sides speak different languages things are still easier for bilingual politicians. In the United States, the national media are weaker. There is no national press, and the things a Congressman says in Washington are less likely to be read in his home district — and vice versa — than would be the case in Britain. Two important studies (Mayhew 1974, Fenno 1978) have recently explored Congressmen's 'home style'. Mayhew classed the activities of re-election-seeking Congressmen under three headings: *advertising, credit-claiming* and *position-taking.* Advertising is best when non-political: commencement speeches, helping with school essay projects (or, more bizarrely, diving to help recover the bodies of drowned constituents — p. 51). All activities helping constituents with bureaucracy or providing highly localised benefits (dams, post offices) are valuable for credit-claiming. Finally, position-taking: if possible, in ways that antagonize nobody: 'The great Polish scientist Copernicus has been unjustly neglected' (p. 62). Fenno followed eighteen Congressmen round their districts listening to their discussions with constituents. His sample covered both parties and a wide range of views, and of types of district. Much of their work was non-political. If a politician can retain his constituents' affection by spending a lot of time with them and being interested in the things they are interested in, they may never ask awkward questions about how he voted. But this does have a cost: time. In spite of a steadily increasing workload on Capitol Hill, almost all the sample spent more time in their districts than was formerly customary. Constituents make more demands on their congressmen than they used to, and politicians who want to be re-elected every two years must respond to them.

When talk turned to politics, Fenno found few cases of outright contradiction. His sample did not so much say incompatible things in Washington and their districts as say different things. When constituents complained about the policies that emerged from Congress, every one of the eighteen blamed Congress itself. Fenno was astonished at how disloyal his sample seemed: 'Members of Congress run *for* Congress by running *against* Congress. The strategy is ubiquitous, addictive, cost-free, and foolproof' (p. 168). But there is no real paradox here. Members may indeed be very loyal to Congress as an institution, but the place to say so is in Congress, not at home. It cuts no ice in Main Street, USA, to say that politics is a process of complex bargaining; that Congress is where it happens; and that every competent Congressman wins some and loses some. Main Street, USA, is interested in the welfare of Main Street, USA, and when it is disappointed it wants to know why. The most painless way is to blame Congress itself.

Readers may feel that all of this shows only that all politicians are liars and crooks. Some are; but not all. Somebody has to produce results when the people will the end but not the means. For instance, most people want there to be gipsy sites and dumps for industrial waste. But nobody wants them in his back garden. In these common circumstances, politicians have to decide to put the gipsy site somewhere, and buy off the enraged neighbours with a promise of some other reward. A messy and inglorious business, no doubt; but nobody has suggested a better way of doing it in a democracy, given that even the most fervent advocates of leaving it all to the market accept that there are some goods that the unfettered market will not provide. For this at least of their tasks, politicians can expect more kicks than ha'pence.

That is one reason why entrepreneurship can never be a complete explanation of why people go into politics. Something beyond the desire to make a profit is needed to explain why people go into such an unpopular occupation. And our examination of the costs of election showed that while politicians can sometimes find others willing to pay these, there rarely is anything left over from which politicians can make a profit. To be sure, ideological entrepreneurs are seeking not just a profit, but implementation of a policy they want. But not all of those who support a policy are prepared to become politicians in order to bring it about. In the last resort, we cannot do without 'expressive' explanations of why people go into politics.

9

The search for love

If it is lonely at the top, it is because it is the lonely who seek to climb there.

H. B. Berrington, 1974, reviewing Iremonger (1970)

Franklin Delano Roosevelt mightily enjoyed being President of the USA (Barber 1977, ch. 7). Having said that, we are almost at the end of an explanatory road. Economists, who made the tools used in Chapter 8, would say that explanation stops right there. There is no accounting for tastes. Some people like Neapolitan ice cream and others like being President. The analyst's job is not to inquire why people have the tastes they have but, given the tastes, to explain what happens as a consequence of people's pursuit of them.

There is a lot to be said for this brisk approach. The benefits of high office are so obvious that perhaps only a psychologist would ever think of asking why people want them. Of course, there are also costs. You don't (usually) get so rich from politics as from land speculation; you may often have to tell lies and disappoint people; an election may suddenly whip all the trappings away from you. But every other nice thing has its costs, too. You don't become an international sportsman without becoming very tired and sore during training; and you have to control your food, drink and sex life very carefully. But nobody thinks it odd that some people want to become international sportsmen. Some people, abnormally tough and clever but not unusual in other respects, have become successful politicians and enjoyed it: for example both Roosevelts and Truman in the USA, and Lloyd George and Harold Wilson in the UK.

But ten minutes' study of politics reveals that there are politicians who do not fit this pattern at all. Everybody who knew Woodrow Wilson knew that he was driven by some powerful inner compulsion. A female friend put it: 'His appreciation of an affection given him was out of the ordinary as was his need of personal love' (quoted in George and George 1956, p. 32). Was this connected with the extraordinary self-destructive rigidity of his behaviour on two or three famous occasions? He threw away the chance of getting what was dearest to him in 1919-20, namely United States membership of the League of Nations. Wilson well knew that the President's power was the power to persuade, and that he could not coerce a reluctant Congress. He had pointed that out himself, as the author of an important book on Congressional government. Nowhere was this truer than in negotiating a treaty, which the Constitution specifies must be approved by a two-thirds vote in the Senate. But over the League of Nations Wilson totally refused to make any compromises in order to get his two-thirds vote, although he had been agile and flexible many times before in his political career. By his behaviour, he lost his own cause. Nobody else could have done it for him.

The downfall of Richard Nixon has more in common with that of Woodrow Wilson than appears at first sight. Of course there were enormous differences between the moral outlooks of the two men. But there were some background resemblances. Both grew up feeling unloved, and sought political office as a compensation. Both stuck grimly to a course of conduct long after it was obvious to everybody else that all was lost: in Wilson's case salvaging the League of Nations, in Nixon's salvaging Richard M. Nixon. Likewise, Lyndon Johnson persevered in escalating the Vietnam war in the face of overwhelming evidence that it was gaining nothing and losing thousands of lives. Does this too bear a psychological explanation? Perhaps. Though probably not as unhappy as Wilson, Johnson enjoyed the Presidency much less than his entrepreneurial triumph as Senate Majority Leader in the 1950s, and wistfully envied Harry Truman his ability to take big decisions and not agonize about them (Kearns 1976, p. 349).

Many politicians in Britain seem to have had similarly unhappy backgrounds. The typical British Prime Minister was bereaved in childhood, hated his public school where he detested games of any sort, especially team games, entered politics to bolster his damaged self-esteem, and then found the top of the greasy pole as lonely and friendless a place as everywhere on the way up (Berrington 1974). The following Prime Ministers since 1832 are recognisable from the above identikit, in all or most of its features: Peel, Russell, Salisbury, Rosebery, Balfour, Asquith, Bonar Law, MacDonald, Chamberlain, Churchill, Eden and Heath.

It is striking how many successful politicians hate, and do badly, precisely the things which they are supposed to love, and do well. They are supposed to be gregarious characters who get elected by glad-handing their voters and get things done by glad-handing their colleagues. But in fact many are shy, lonely introverts who hate canvassing and loathe kissing babies. Three leading Conservatives (one of them now ex-), alike in nothing else, can stand as examples. Enoch Powell: his 'worst ordeal was the need to knock on door after door "cold" and make conversation with strangers he was trying to convert into supporters' (A. Roth, quoted in Berrington 1974, p. 361). Sir Keith Joseph: a pathologically shy man whose canvassing technique in 1979 was to wait until there were no shoppers in the shop he was visiting, so that nobody would be inconvenienced. Sir Ian Gilmour: 'not a good campaigner, being too shy and self-effacing. Glad-handing in market squares has never been his forté'.[1] The examples could be taken from any party.

There are other unlikely politicians: those who got where they did apparently by accident and who did the job out of a sense of duty. Prime Ministers who fit this pattern include Lord Melbourne ('I think it's a damned bore. I am in many minds as to what to do' — quoted in Berrington 1974, p. 365) and Sir Alec Douglas-Home. American Presidents who fit it include William Taft, Calvin Coolidge, and Dwight D. Eisenhower. Accidental politicians who did not enjoy themselves, like the lonely neurotics, cannot intelligibly be called entrepreneurs.

It is tempting to try to classify the behaviour of politicians like these, collect information about their backgrounds and tie the two together into a psychological explanation. Much of this must rely, though, on rather unreliable sources: one cannot interview past politicians, and can only study their own and their friends' statements about their job satisfaction.

Several hypotheses have been constructed, of which the best known are Freudian, but the most illuminating come from writers who propose more flexible causal relationships. There is obviously too little material to make out a strong case for a single psychological syndrome and in many cases we have to be content with descriptions of the individuals rather than attempt systematic explanations.

For many people, psychological explanations of behaviour are too closely linked to that scientific fraud Sigmund Freud, who contributed to a psychobiography of Woodrow Wilson which is one of the worst history books ever written (Freud and Bullitt 1967). Freudians make their points far too easily. If a politician says he hated his father, that is evidence that he did; but if he says he loved his father, that is evidence of a 'reaction-formation': he really did hate him. When Woodrow Wilson once spoke of his regard for somebody whom, according to Freud and Bullitt, he hated, they comment 'These remarks seem authentic, and the contradiction they involve seems to be evidence merely of a disturbed mental condition' (p. 255). As it is impossible to argue with this sort of thing, it is perhaps best to let it alone.

But not all psychological explanations of behaviour are Freudian; and even the Freudian ones may have some truth in them, though there seems to be no way of finding out whether they do. But there is a core of hard fact in search of an explanation. British Prime Ministers *are* more likely to have been bereaved in childhood than any comparable group in the population. Woodrow Wilson *did* behave in an extraordinary way in 1919-20. The most sustained and convincing attempt at general classification is J. D. Barber's (1977 — first published 1972) study of the eleven US Presidents from Taft (1909-13) to Nixon (1969-74).[2] In this work, Barber moved on from the classifications of *The Lawmakers* (1965 — see Chapter 6 above) to one that is perhaps more pessimistic. The Connecticut lawmakers included people with both high and low self-esteem; amongst the Presidents, the former seem rarer, including only Roosevelt, Truman and Kennedy. Advertisers do not feature in the newer book; one would scarcely take advertisement for one's law practice to the length of becoming President. (But one might start out as an Advertiser before being drawn to stay in for other reasons. John B. Anderson ran for Winnebago County, Ill., State's Attorney in 1956 because 'Having newly re-established my practice, and being barred by the canons of ethics from advertising for clients, the campaign provided, win or lose, an excellent means of putting my name and qualifications before the public'.[3] That road led eventually to his independent Presidential candidature in 1980). But the Spectator and the Reluctant, as well as the Lawmaker, survive in Barber's new categorisation. He divides Presidents according to two cross-cutting criteria, giving four types. One criterion is activity-passivity, which just means the amount of energy the President invests in his job. The second is 'positive-negative affect towards one's activity', which refers to whether he enjoys it or not. Some Presidents fit into each box, as in Figure 9.1.

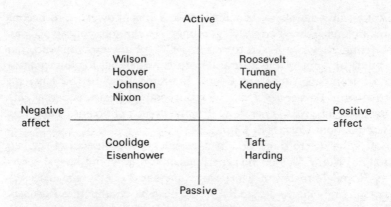

Figure 9.1 Barber's classification of US Presidents
Source: Summarised from Barber (1977), chs. 1-10

Several critics (e.g. George 1974, Elms 1976) have pointed out that this classification is merely descriptive, not explanatory, and that the underlying psychological theories are not sufficiently spelt out. Nevertheless. Barber's divisions are useful because they group politicians in a way that demonstrates that people of quite different attitudes may have similar reasons for being in politics. The psychologically interesting side of Figure 9.1 is the left-hand one. Of people who enjoy politics, we need only add that they may enjoy it passively as well as actively. As of autumn 1981, Ronald Reagan still appears to enjoy being President of the United States, just as Roosevelt did. But it is the being, not the doing, that Reagan enjoys. He seems to be a 'passive-positive'. The nearest British Prime Ministers to fitting this pattern are probably Sir Henry Campbell-Bannerman and Sir Alec Douglas-Home. A list of British active-positives is bound to be controversial, but my twentieth-century candidates are Lloyd George, Baldwin, Attlee and Wilson.

So far, so uncomplicated. 'Positives', whether active or passive, are in politics because they enjoy being there, and there is no need to say any more. But what about the others? Why should anybody voluntarily take part in an activity he dislikes? One reason is civic duty. We came across this in Chapter 4 in the context of voting. Many people vote not because they expect to maximise their utility by voting but because they feel that, as citizens, they ought to vote. And the same is true of some politicians, even at the top. Historians seem to agree that the expressed reluctance of two distinguished

American generals — Washington and Eisenhower — to become
politicians was perfectly genuine. 'I cannot conceive', said
Eisenhower when asked to run in 1948, 'of any circumstance that
could drag out of me permission to consider me for any political
post from dogcatcher to Grand Supreme King of the Universe'
(quoted in Barber 1977, p. 159). But many Americans persistently
believe that great generals will make great politicians. They were
wrong about Ulysses S. Grant.

It is harder to think of a 'passive-negative' politician at the very
top in Britain. Melbourne is perhaps an example; but he last served
as Prime Minister in 1841, and anyway he may have secretly
enjoyed it, whatever he said. Another possible candidate is Rosebery;
but there is no clear case this century. Perhaps this shows that in
Britain generals do not feel the duty to serve but aristocrats do.
(Exam question: Discuss the policies of *either* the Kitchener cabinet
or the Haig cabinet *or* the Montgomery cabinet). The idea of *noblesse
oblige* has survived longer in local than in national government in
Britain. In rural Britain, the Squire traditionally dispensed justice,
and some squires continued to do so after democratic local
government began in the shires in 1889. In the 1960s or 1970s, the
Earl of Macclesfield still governed Oxfordshire, Lord Porchester
Hampshire, and Viscount Ridley Northumberland. The Ridleys
have been governing Northumberland in the Conservative interest,
on and off, since 1832, and the present Viscount inherited both his
title and his seat on the County Council from his father. Not all of
these are passive-negatives. But some certainly have been, especially
in the days when it was part of the Squire's job to govern the
county, as it was part of his wife's to distribute charity to the
deserving poor. Nevertheless, local government has gradually
passed, even in rural areas, from 'social leaders' to 'public persons'
whose social status comes only from their service on the council (see
Lee 1963, *passim*).

The 'active-negatives' are psychologically more interesting still.
British leaders in this category include Salisbury, Asquith,
Chamberlain, and Eden. They have nothing in common except that
they did not enjoy the exercise of power. One may say briskly that
many of them had good reason to be unhappy as they were inefficient
or incompetent. But not all were: Salisbury, for instance, was a
highly successful Prime Minister, but that does not seem to have
made him a happy one.

The leading studies of unhappy Presidents (George and George 1956; Kearns 1976) are more or less Freudian. Woodrow Wilson had a terrifying, sarcastic father and a 'rather plain, extremely reserved' mother. As an adult, Woodrow[4] remembered 'how I clung to her (a laughed-at "mama's boy") till I was a great big fellow'. The Freudian interpretation of this is labelled 'Oedipus complex'. The boy loves his mother and wants to kill his father. He cannot publicly express his hatred of his father; indeed by reaction he may (as Woodrow Wilson did) stress how much he loves or admires him. But the more he represses his hatred for his father, the more it comes to dominate his behaviour, which becomes rigid and compulsive. Unable to kill his real father, the Oedipal adult vents his bottled-up, unreasoning hatred on a substitute. Wilson encountered a father-figure twice — in Dean West of Princeton University and in US Senator Henry Cabot Lodge. The latter was the object of Wilson's final self-destructive fight. He led the 'irreconcilable' faction in the Congress which was not prepared to have the League of Nations at any price. In manner, he was overbearing and sarcastic — he once said that Wilson's oratory might pass muster at Princeton, but not at Harvard.[5] Because of his passionate will to resist his 'father', Wilson refused all compromise on the League issue with those who were willing to compromise: it would have been giving in to the enemy. He would rather (and did) lose everything rather than make any concession to the authority-figure he hated above all.

Lyndon Johnson's father was inadequate for different reasons: a drunken and improvident small-town Texas politician who neglected his child and had no interest in his wife's sad little efforts to bring culture to their dusty outback ranch. In adult life, Lyndon Johnson was an outstanding political entrepreneur — the last person ever to get the Senate Democrats to work together as if they belonged to a political party — but there was an unhappy, compulsive streak to his character which became more prominent as he became Vice-President and then President. He was good at managing one-to-one encounters where he felt he could give and (he hoped) receive affection, but bad at dealing with large groups. He was a compulsive present-giver; while working on her biography of him, Kearns got twelve electric toothbrushes (on separate occasions, not all at once). And in the great crisis of his Presidency — Vietnam — he showed a rigidity that has often been compared to Woodrow Wilson's as he refused to admit that the escalation of the war was a total failure.[6]

However, Oedipus complexes do not get us very far. If the Freudian model fits Wilson (and it does seem to), it surely cannot also fit Johnson, whose parents and background were so different to Wilson's, and whose adult behaviour had only the final obstinate rigidity in common. A better explanation would start from the accepted fact of emotional deprivation in childhood and draw less ambitious but more general conclusions.

According to Karen Horney's (1937) study of the 'neurotic personality', 'the basic evil is invariably a lack of genuine warmth and affection in childhood' (p. 80). This tends to make people neurotic as adults: that is, abnormally anxious, rigid in their behaviour and disposed to underestimate their own good qualities. The neurotic may seek a way out in a constant search for affection or for power, or in submissiveness or withdrawal (pp. 96-99). There are many ways whereby a child may be deprived of its parents' affection: illegitimacy (Ramsay MacDonald), bereavement (Salisbury), remote unfeeling parent(s) (Churchill, Woodrow Wilson), weak inadequate ones (Johnson, Nixon). It would be absurd to believe that all these conditions led children to hate their fathers and love their mothers; but it is not absurd to believe that they are disposed to compensate for the affection they never got in childhood by one or more of the routes Horney suggests. Those who choose submissiveness and/or withdrawal are unlikely to become politicians; those who choose love and/or power (even though they may conflict) are likely to become politicians, even if their shy natures are thereby exposed to a severe battering.

This is at the same time a weaker and a stronger theory than Freud's. Weaker, because it does not make so clear a prediction of how the subject will behave. But also stronger, because it covers so many more cases. Tucker (1977) points out that Woodrow Wilson can be fully explained in terms of a Horneyan search for love (primarily) and power (secondarily). He was very deeply touched by his tumultuous reception from the crowds in Paris in 1919. The people loved him, he thought. He was the Great Peacemaker, and if only he could impose his will (? power) on a few cross-grained politicians like Lloyd George and Clemenceau and Lodge, they would love him for ever. Iremonger's thesis, and especially Berrington's reworking of it, draw much more Horneyan than Freudian conclusions from the bereavement of British Prime

Ministers. Salisbury, MacDonald and Churchill had utterly different backgrounds. They were not all bereaved, but they were certainly all emotionally deprived. They were not even all classic introverts (Churchill, for instance, compensated for his emotional deprivation and physical frailty by bursts of frantic, unreflective activity). But they all seem to have been profoundly lonely. No less than any other occupational group, many politicians seem to lead lives of quiet desperation. It may indeed be true that it is lonely at the top because it is the lonely who get there.

None of this implies that all politicians are crazy, or even that neurotic leaders are always bad leaders. Not every future Prime Minister is deprived in childhood, and writers like Iremonger would be more credible if they did not try so hard to bend the obviously well-adjusted (Lloyd George, Attlee) into their favourite pattern, and also if they could get down to the work of putting their studies on a proper statistical basis, for instance by comparing Prime Ministers both with people in politics but not at the top and with people at the top but not in politics. And an active-positive type does not always make the best President or Prime Minister, especially in the eyes of those who think that 'he governs best who governs least'. In the end, the claim that F. D. Roosevelt was a 'better' President than Calvin Coolidge rests on a value-judgement about what a 'good' President ought to do. Furthermore, different temperaments suit different times. Harry Truman was arguably very well suited to be President at the time he was. He had to take some agonizing decisions: dropping the A-bombs on Hiroshima and Nagasaki, for instance, and sacking General Douglas MacArthur. He thought; he decided; having decided, he went to bed; and that was that for one of the least introspective Presidents in US history. On the other hand, as Storr (1969) argues, it is perhaps just as well that Churchill was not like that. A cool well-adjusted rational man might have accepted Hitler's offer of negotiated peace in 1940 in the absence of any hard evidence that Britain could fight on alone. (Churchill, of all people, cannot have known in May 1940 that Britain would survive because of her superior radar; his pet scientist, F. A. Lindemann, was actively obstructing its development — see e.g. Snow 1962). Only somebody who needed action to keep his depression at bay would have considered fighting on against hopeless odds.

Even somebody like Woodrow Wilson who ends up by destroying

himself may have had the dynamism to do a great deal of good earlier on. The risk with a neurotic leader is that he may be crippled at a vital time by some excessive anxiety, provoking a disproportionate response to some trivial incident, or a rigid pursuit of a doomed policy, or a collapse of his relationships with colleagues and subordinates. On the other hand, if people with abnormally strong needs did not come forward, political offices would be hard to staff. Most people do prefer cultivating their gardens, after all; and, as the previous chapter has shown that we cannot expect entrepreneurs to do it all, there will always remain a need for people who enter politics to satisfy their psychological needs.

Conclusion

This book has had two missionary aims: to show that rival approaches to the study of political behaviour are complementary, not incompatible, and that voters, politicians and intermediaries of various kinds are not as stupid or as narrow-minded as they are sometimes made out to be.

There is no substitute for survey research. Nothing else gives as accurate a picture of what the voters think is important, and of what they think should be done about it. So long as we do not mistakenly infer anything from the opinions they express on policies which do not matter to them, we can then go on to examine what politicians offer in the light of what the voters want. In general, they do offer more or less what the median voter wants, as the deductive theory would predict. When they fail to do that (Goldwater, McGovern, Thatcher, Benn), the voters are likely to reject them in favour of other politicians who do.

This simple message is of course hedged around with restrictions. If the reader has found some chapters hard going, I hope he will accept that I have tried to present both a simple basic position and some of the quite complex modifications necessary to adapt it to a complex real world. The basic position itself reflects a value-judgment which I believe the evidence justifies: that voters are not stupid. In this I share the views of V. O. Key, whose posthumously published *The Responsible Electorate* (1966) vigorously defended voters from the then-fashionable charges of ignorance and apathy. Empirical evidence to support him was scanty in his time; and the Downsians, who never did believe that voters were stupid, were working in isolation from the empirical researchers, some of whom believed too readily that they were. Neither of these restrictions still holds; and this book has attempted to show students where the balance of scholarly opinion now lies.

As well as believing that voters are not stupid, I confess to a second prejudice: that politics is not a contemptible occupation. Some of those who go into politics do so for self-serving reasons; but that is neither surprising nor to be condemned, unless we condemn the butcher, the baker and the candlestickmaker for doing the same. And some politicians are engaged in the altruistic provision of public goods. In the process they may get their hands dirty with grubby log-rolling and messy bargains. It is just as well for the rest of us that they are prepared to.

Notes

CHAPTER 1: VOTING: THREE APPROACHES

1 In the 1979 General Election, the Conservatives made dramatic gains in rural Wales. But this did not erase the patterns discussed in this paragraph; the Conservatives even then polled less in rural Wales than in comparable agricultural seats elsewhere.

2 For more about centre-periphery politics, see Lipset and Rokkan (1967), McLean (1977), Guthrie and McLean (1978), and Steed (1979).

3 But see Miller (1977) for a sophisticated treatment of aggregate British data since 1918 which avoids the traps discussed in this chapter.

4 If the Democrats had not split, they would have had ten per cent more of the popular vote than Lincoln, but still lost the election. This is because the Electoral College system rewards candidates who can get a narrow majority in many or populous states and penalises those who run up big majorities in one area. Lincoln narrowly beat Douglas all over the North; the Democrats piled up huge majorities (and united would have piled up huger ones) in the South. The candidate with most votes in a state normally wins all that state's electoral votes; Lincoln's 39.9 per cent of the popular vote secured him 180 out of 283 (63.6 per cent) of the votes in the Electoral College.

5 For an ecological analysis of Southern voting which has less sweep but far more detail than Lipset's, see Key (1949): the only English-language work on electoral geography fit to rank with Siegfried. See for instance the intriguing electoral maps of Tennessee, 1860--1944, on p. 77.

6 Butler and Stokes (1974), p. 191.

7 *Washington Post,* 21 September 1980.

8 Michael Wheeler, 'Reining in horserace journalism', *Public Opinion,* Feb.--Mar. 1980, p. 42.

9 All figures in this paragraph are from ICPSR, *1980 CPS election study: January--February pre-election interviews* (Ann Arbor, University of Michigan, 1980).

CHAPTER 2: THE BRITISH VOTER

1   R. W. Burchfield, *The Spoken Word: A Guide to Preferred Usage,*
    quoted in *The Guardian,* 21 March 1981.

2   'Total-vote' or 'Butler' rather than 'two-party' or 'Steed' swing.

3   'Immigrants' is inaccurate, of course; the question really refers to
    coloured native British citizens. But the first is still a popular code
    phrase for the second.

4   *The Economist,* 13 December 1980, p. 54.

CHAPTER 3: THE AMERICAN VOTER

1   'Creation vs Evolution: Battle Resumes in Public Schools'. *Washington
    Post,* 13 September 1980.

2   Sources for Table 3.2: 1974 voting figure: US Bureau of the Census
    (1976), Table 732. 1980 voting figures: *Washington Post,* 6 November
    1980. 'Targeted' liberals: Sens. Bayh (Ind.), Church (Idaho), Cranston
    (Calif.), Culver (Iowa), Eagleton (Mo.), McGovern (S.D.). As listed by
    Terry Dolan, chairman of the National Conservative Political Action
    Committee, *Washington Post,* 12 November 1980. Non-targeted
    liberals: Sens. Hart (Colo.), Leahy (Vt), Nelson (Wisc.). Others: All
    others except La (no contest in 1980), Ala. and Hawaii (no R. candidate
    in 1974).
    The 'Other' figure in Table 3.2 is inflated by Ark. and Ga., where the
    Democratic vote slumped as part of the general decline of the party in
    the South. If these contests are excluded, the 'other' figure drops to 3.3
    per cent.

3   Surveys show that fundamentalists differ from the mean only in their
    attitude to religious questions in politics, and not on all of those.
    Public Opinion April–May 1981, pp. 20-27, 41.

4   Survey by Prof. Larry Sabato, University of Virginia, reported in
    Washington Post, 28 October 1980.

5   1976 figure from Nie *et al.* (1979), pp. 383-5; 1980 figure from ABC
    exit poll, *Washington Post,* 6 November 1980.

6   Both questions from the 'Cross of Gold' speech are as cited in Morison
    et al. (1969), p. 190.

7   Ironically, they lost in 1876. The Republicans had a majority of one in
    the Electoral College.

8   For example, Sen. Gary Hart (D. -Colo.) See his 'Democrats: A New
    Path to Old Goals', *Washington Post,* 23 September 1980.

CHAPTER 4: THE RATIONAL CHOICE APPROACH

1 Many middle-class liberals thought that Carter had won. The electorate disagreed. A survey in Virginia found that 53 per cent of those who had watched the debate thought that Reagan had won it whereas only 12 per cent thought Carter had. G. Joy, J. Pieper, W. Davis and D. Magleby, 'Explaining the 1980 Presidential vote in Virginia: the results of a state-wide panel study', paper for the 1980 meeting of the Virginia Political Science Association, December 1980. See also Ware (1981).

2 After attending a rally addressed by George Bush in Roanoke, Va., in October 1980, I read the following message on a hand-drying machine in the toilet: 'Push the button for a message from your Congressman'.

3 I am very grateful to Michael Laver, who first gave me this example. I have simplified the story he told me, but I hope it preserves the ring of truth.

4 It has a colourful history. The first person writing in English to discover it was Lewis Carroll, who did not know of Condorcet's work. See Black (1958), which reprints some of Lewis Carroll's pamphlets.

5 The most accessible of Arrow's own presentations is Arrow (1967). Two relatively simple, but not simple-minded, discussions are Mueller (1979) chs. 2, 3, and 10 (but there is a mistake in the proof on p. 187), and Plott (1976).

CHAPTER 5: PRESSURE GROUPS

1 (British Telecoms, from 1980).

2 The distributors of 'rapacious benevolence' in Dickens's *Bleak House.*

3 These words (from the Second Amendment to the US Constitution) may suggest that the NRA has the Constitution on its side. But the Supreme Court has ruled that the second part of the Amendment is dependent on the first: that is, that the right to bear arms applies to those who join a state militia, not to the whole population. See *Presser vs Illinois*, 116 US 252 and *US vs Miller,* 307 US 174 (1939). The National Firearms Act 1934 had outlawed interstate commerce in sawn-off shotguns; in *US vs Miller* the Supreme Court refused to strike down the Act under the Second Amendment because it held that the Act did not interfere with the constitutional right of states to raise a militia.

4 So called because it reinstates the view that élites rule, and not of course because it favours rule by élites. It is a clumsy label, which was pinned on the 'élitists' by other people.

CHAPTER 6: PARTY ACTIVISTS

1 *Washington Post,* 23 September 1980.
2 Interview, Gary Hart, Grand Junction, Colo., 27 September 1980.
3 Interview, Willard Leavel, Denver, 26 September 1980.
4 Quoted in McKenzie 1964, p. 7 (Hartington), p. 176 (Salisbury).
5 Rose's own, by now rather dated, evidence comes from a study of all resolutions submitted to the Labour and Conservative Annual Conferences from 1955 to 1960 inclusive. Many of them merely called for what everybody in the party, or indeed everybody in the country, wanted (and, of course, people who propose resolutions asking for something to be done are not forced to say who must pay for it). Of those which did not, left-wing Labour proposals outnumbered right-wing ones by 893 to 35; right-wing Conservative proposals outnumbered left-wing ones by 505 to 62. Resolutions calling for what everybody wants in any case are a form of expressivism. They are not evidence that ideological activists are as likely to be 'moderate' as 'extreme'. Professor Rose also cites three other studies (p. 208). Two of these offer no support for his conclusion, and the third runs directly counter to it.
   Up-to-date evidence of the gulf between Labour activists' views and Labour supporters' can be found in numerous reputable surveys. See, e.g., *Daily Express,* 7 February 1979; *The Times* 17 January 1980; *Sunday Times* 31 August 1980; Whiteley and Gordon (1980); Crewe (1981); and a plethora of polls in September 1981, which showed that Labour voters strongly preferred Denis Healey to Tony Benn for the Deputy Leadership of the party, while activists preferred the reverse. The documentation for the Conservatives is, unfortunately, less full because researchers and journalists are less fascinated by 'unrepresentativeness' on the right than on the left.
6 The best account of Baldwin's troubles is Ramsden (1978), ch. 13, from which come all quotations in this paragraph, except the last, which is from McKenzie (1964), p. 143.
7 The first quotation is from Attlee (1937), p. 93; the second is a letter from Attlee to Harold Laski on 20 August 1945, as quoted in Butler and Sloman (1980), p. 250.

CHAPTER 7: BUREAUCRATS

1 Mill (1972), p. 246 (*Representative Government*); cf. also p. 166 (*On Liberty*). Rowland Hill was an inventive aristocrat who in 1840 persuaded a reluctant Post Office to adopt the idea of prepaid stamps

to stick on letters. Previously postage was paid willy-nilly by the unfortunate recipient.

2   Gerth and Mills 1948, p. 228. But Weber was not as careful an observer as most people think; he claimed (p. 240) that 'the French, English and American bureaucracies have for a long time forgone [entry] examinations . . ., for training and service in party organisations have made up for them'. As regards the USA, the comment is fair; as regards France and Britain it is preposterous.

3   Parliamentary Private Secretary — a junior MP on the government side who acts as unpaid assistant to the minister.

4   For the 19th century, the charge is certainly fair, as anybody who once had to read the Board of Trade evidence to the Select Committee on Import Duties of 1840 probably remembers. See also Brown (1958). The dedicated free-traders running the Board of Trade were determined to sweep away Britain's (mostly agricultural) protectionism. Competitive examinations may have reinforced this bias if they made it harder for country gentlemen to become administrators. Nowadays, the relevant departments are schizophrenically split between encouraging free trade and trying to persuade other departments to buy British.

5   The main source for these two paragraphs is the author's participant-observation on the fringe of the events they describe. See also Kellner and Crowther-Hunt (1980), ch. 9.

6   Though some crusaders (e.g. Niskanen 1971, chs. 19-21) forget that market solutions must be policed. A voucher system for education may merely shift the locus of bureaucracy from officials allocating children to schools to inspectors checking against illegal use or forgery of education vouchers.

7   *Times Higher Education Supplement*, 6 February 1981. The paper recommended that polytechnic grants should be channelled through one, nominally independent, 'buffer' body; the real intention was that there should be only one channel for government money, so that it could be cut more effectively. The Emperor Nero wished that the Roman people had only one neck.

8   For the most recent, marvellously hypocritical, restatement of the politicians' position, see Cmnd 7982 (1980): *The Government's Reply to the First Special Report of the Select Committee on Education, Science and the Arts, Session 1979—80.* The reply, to a request to see documents about inter-departmental rows, was shorter than the title of the document.

CHAPTER 8: ENTREPRENEURS

1   Because a citizen could exploit his fellows by refusing to give his agreement under the unanimity rule. He would gain more by selling his vote in this way than by voting 'sincerely' for the power to tax to provide the public good. But everybody can play that game. So nobody would vote for the power to tax. So you need a vote to force everybody to vote sincerely. But somebody might strategically refuse to support that proposal in turn . . .

2   *The Times,* 27 August 1976.

3   'West Virginia's Deep Pockets', *Washington Post,* 29 November 1980. In terms of expenditure per vote at constant prices, this is still well below 19th century British levels -- e.g. at the Oxford by-election of 1880.

4   'Republicans Winning the Battle of Bucks', *Washington Post,* 9 October 1980.

5   '25 House Races Broke Spending Records, and the Meter's Running', *Washington Post,* 8 November 1980.

6   'Voters may be Turning off but PAC Money Faucets are Gushing', *Washington Post,* 25 and 26 October 1980.

7   'A Rare Bird is Sighted Flying from Capitol Hill', *Washington Post,* 5 October 1980.

8   'Lawmaker and Silver Tycoon Help Each Other', *Washington Post,* 3 October 1980.

9   Buckley vs. Valeo, 424 US 1 (1976).

10 'IRS Reverses Itself, Will Allow Groups' "Report Cards" on Legislators', *Washington Post,* 9 October 1980.

11 No doubt it was only seeming. Consumers paid in the end, by way of auto prices and/or subsidies to lossmaking companies. But it is the seeming that matters. If the benefits of a policy are conspicuous and the costs hidden, it is not surprising if it is popular.

12 L. Atherley-Jones, MP, quoted in Clegg, Fox and Thompson (1964), p. 364.

13 This account is derived from Clegg *et al.* (1964), chs. 8 and 10, and from the *House of Commons Hansard* for the relevant dates.

14 There is no room here for an adequate discussion of the problem or of Beveridge's solution. See Braithwaite (1957), Titmuss (1958), and Harris (1977).

15 This account is derived from Harris (1977), chs. 16 and 17, and Addison (1975), chs. VI and VIII to X.

16 'Public good' is a technical term. Neither here nor anywhere else in this book do I mean to imply that I think the objective was valuable, merely that a substantial number of people did and that it had the characteristics of indivisibility and non-excludability discussed in Chapter 4.

CHAPTER 9: THE SEARCH FOR LOVE

1 'The aristocrat with a licence to be wet', *The Guardian* 21 June 1980.

2 The second edition contains profiles of Carter and Ford that are necessarily more superficial than the material in the first edition.

3 Quoted in 'Anderson: Steady, Self-confident and Purposefully Well-rounded', *Washington Post* 23 October 1980.

4 Thomas Woodrow Wilson, James Ramsay MacDonald and James Keir Hardie have two things in common. Each lacked an affectionate father (the two British politicians were both illegitimate children who never met their fathers); and each, in adolescence, dropped his given Christian name in favour of his mother's maiden name which was his middle name. Even those who dislike psychohistory may be tempted to admit that something unusual is going on here.

5 Wilson had been President of Princeton; Lodge, a member of an aristocratic New England dynasty, had been at Harvard.

6 Ironically but irrelevantly, Johnson too was dealing with a Henry Cabot Lodge; but his was on the same side, as US Ambassador in Saigon.

Bibliography

Notes:-- 1) Books published in both the UK and the USA are listed as follows:

If published under separate titles, both titles are given.

If published with separate imprints, the British publisher is given.

If published by the same publisher, his headquarters are given as place of publication.

2) Abbreviations of journals, etc;

AEI	American Enterprise Institute for Public Policy Research
AJPS	American Journal of Political Science
APSR	American Political Science Review
BJPS	British Journal of Political Science
HMSO	Her Majesty's Stationery Office
ICPSR	Inter-university Consortium for Political and Social Research
IEA	Institute of Economic Affairs
JP	Journal of Politics
PA	Parliamentary Affairs
PS	Political Studies
WP	World Politics

Abrams, R. (1980) *Foundations of Political Analysis: An Introduction to the Theory of Collective Choice* New York, Columbia University Press.

Addison, P. (1975) *The Road to 1945: British Politics and the Second World War* London, Jonathan Cape.

Albrow, M. (1970) *Bureaucracy* London, Pall Mall

American Political Science Association (1950) 'Towards a More Responsible Two-party System', supplement to *APSR* XLIV.

Andersen, K. (1979) *The Creation of a Democratic Majority 1928-36* Chicago, University of Chicago Press.

Arrow, K. J. (1967) 'Values and Collective Decision-making' in P. Laslett and W. G. Runciman (eds) *Philosophy, Politics, and Society, Third Series* Oxford, Blackwell, pp. 215-32.

Attlee, C. R. (1937) *The Labour Party in Perspective* London, Gollancz.

Bachrach, P. and Baratz, M. S. (1962) 'Two faces of power' *APSR*, LVI, 4, pp. 947-52.

Barber, J. D. (1965) *The Lawmakers: Recruitment and Adaptation to Legislative Life* New Haven, Conn., Yale UP.

Barber, J. D. (1977) *The Presidential Character: Predicting Performance in the White House* (2nd edn) Englewood Cliffs, NJ., Prentice-Hall.

Barry, B. M. (1970) *Sociologists, Economists and Democracy* London, Collier-Macmillan.

Bealey, F. and Pelling, H.M. (1958) *Labour and Politics 1900-06* London, Macmillan.

Beer, S. H. (1965) *Modern British Politics* London, Faber & Faber. Published in the USA as *British Politics in the Collectivist Age* New York, NY., Alfred A. Knopf.

Benney, M., Gray, A., and Pear, R. (1956) *How People Vote* London, Routledge

Berelson, B. R., Lazarsfeld, P. F., and McPhee, W. N. (1954) *Voting: A study of Opinion Formation in a Presidential Campaign* Chicago, Ill., University of Chicago Press.

Bish, G. (1979) 'Drafting the Manifesto' in K. Coates (ed) *What went Wrong: explaining the fall of the Labour Government* Nottingham, Spokesman, pp. 187-206.

Black, D. (1958) *The Theory of Committees and Elections* Cambridge, Cambridge UP.

Blalock, H. M. (1960) *Social Statistics* New York, NY, McGraw-Hill.

Blewett, N. (1972) *The Peers, the Parties and the People: the General Elections of 1910* London, Macmillan.

Borrow, G. (1977) *Wild Wales* Glasgow, Fontana. First published in 1862.

Bradley, I. (1981) *Breaking the Mould? The Birth and Prospects of the Social Democratic Party* Oxford, Martin Robertson.

Braithwaite, W. J. (1957) *Lloyd George's Ambulance Wagon* London, Methuen.

Brams, S. J. (1976) *Paradoxes in Politics: An Introduction to the Nonobvious in Political Science* New York, NY, The Free Press.

Brittan, S. (1971) *Steering the Economy: the Role of the Treasury* Harmondsworth, Penguin.

Brittan, S. (1975) 'The Economic Contradictions of Democracy' *BJPS* V, 2, pp. 129-60.

Brown, L. (1958) *The Board of Trade and the Free Trade Movement 1830-42* Oxford, Clarendon Press.

Butler, D. E. and Kavanagh, D. (1980) *The British General Election of 1979* London, Macmillan.

Butler, D. E. and Sloman, A. (1980) *British Political Facts* (5th edn) London, Macmillan.

Butler, D. E. and Stokes, D. (1974) *Political Change in Britain* (2nd edn) London, Macmillan.

Campbell, A., Converse, P. E., Miller, W. E., and Stokes, D. (1960) *The American Voter* New York, NY., Wiley.

Campbell, A., Converse, P. E., Miller, W. E., and Stokes, D. (1966) *Elections and the Political Order* New York, NY., Wiley

Chapman, L. (1979) *Your Disobedient Servant* (2nd edn) Harmondsworth, Penguin.

Clegg, H. A., Fox, A., and Thompson, A. F., (1964) *A History of British Trade Unions since 1889, Vol. I, 1889-1910* Oxford, Clarendon Press.

Converse, P. E. (1964) 'The Nature of Belief Systems in Mass Publics' in D. E. Apter (ed), *Ideology and Discontent* New York, NY, Free Press, pp. 206-61.

Converse, P.E. (1966) 'Religion and Politics: the 1960 Election' in Campbell *et al.* (1966), pp. 96-124.

Cook, C. P. (1976) *A Short History of the Liberal Party 1900-76* London, Macmillan.

Crewe, I. (1981) 'Why the Conservatives Won' in H. R. Penniman (ed) *Britain at the Polls, 1979* Washington, DC, (AEI) pp. 263-305.

Crossman, R. H. S. (1975) *The Diaries of a Cabinet Minister, vol I, Minister of Housing 1964-66* London, Hamish Hamilton and Jonathan Cape.

Dahl, R. A. (1956) *A Preface to Democratic Theory* Chicago, Ill., University of Chicago Press.

Dahl, R. A. (1961) *Who Governs?* New Haven, Conn., Yale UP.

Dahl, R. A. (1971) *Polyarchy* New Haven, Conn., Yale UP.

Dahl, R. A. and Lindblom, C. (1953) *Politics, Economics and Welfare* New York, NY., Harper & Row.

Downs, A. (1957) *An Economic Theory of Democracy* New York, NY., Harper and Row.

Downs, A. (1960) 'Why the Government Budget is Too Small in a Democracy' *WP* XII, 4, pp. 541-64.

Downs, A. (1967) *Inside Bureaucracy* Boston, Mass., Little, Brown & Co.

Dunleavy, P. (1979) 'The Urban Basis of Political Alignment: Social Class, Domestic Property Ownership, and State Intervention in Consumption Processes' *BJPS*, IX, 4, pp. 409-44.

Elms, A. C. (1976) *Personality in Politics* New York, NY., Harcourt Brace.

Fenno, R. F. (1978) *Home Style: House Members in their Districts* Boston, Mass., Little, Brown & Co.

Finer, S. E. (ed.) (1975) *Adversary Politics and Electoral Reform* London, Anthony Wigram.

Finer, S. E. (1980) *The Changing British Party System 1945-79* Washington, DC, AEI.

Freud, S. and Bullitt, W. C. (1967) *Thomas Woodrow Wilson, 28th President of the United States: a psychological study* London, Weidenfeld & Nicolson.

Frohlich, N., Oppenheimer, J., and Young, O. (1971) *Political Leadership and Collective Goods* Princeton, NJ., Princeton UP.

Frohlich, N. and Oppenheimer, J. (1978) *Modern Political Economy* Englewood Cliffs, NJ., Prentice-Hall.

Garrett, J. (1980) *Managing the Civil Service* London, Heinemann.

George, A., and George, J. (1956) *Woodrow Wilson and Colonel House: a personality study* New York NY., The John Day Co.

George, A. (1974) 'Assessing Presidential Character' *WP* XXVI, pp. 234-82.

Gerth, H. H. and Mills, C. W. (1948) *From Max Weber: Essays in Sociology* London, Routledge.

Goldthorpe, J. H., Lockwood, D., Bechhofer, F., and Platt, J., (1968) *The Affluent Worker* (3 vols.) London, Cambridge UP.

Guthrie, R. and McLean, I. S. (1978) 'Another Part of the Periphery: Reactions to Devolution in an English Development Area' *PA* XXXI, 2, pp. 190-200.

Hansard Society (1981) *Paying for Politics* London, Hansard Society for Parliamentary Government.

Harris, J. (1977) *William Beveridge: a Biography* Oxford, Clarendon Press.

Harrop, M. (1980) 'The Urban Basis of Political Alignment: a Comment', *BJPS* X, 3, pp. 388-98.

Heclo, H. and Wildavsky, A. (1974) *The Private Government of Public Money: Community and Policy inside British Politics* London, Macmillan.

Hewitt, C. (1974) 'Policy-making in Postwar Britain: A Nation-level Test of Elitist and Pluralist Hypotheses' *BJPS* IV, 2, pp. 187-216.

Hobbes, T. (1968) *Leviathan* Harmondsworth, Penguin ed. (Originally published in 1651).

Hofstadter, R. (1948) *The American Political Tradition and the Men who Made It* New York, NY., Alfred A. Knopf.

Horney, K. (1937) *The Neurotic Personality of our Time* New York, NY., W. W. Norton.

Houghton, Lord (1976) *Report of the Committee on Financial Aid to Political Parties* (chairman Lord Houghton of Sowerby), Cmnd 6601. London, HMSO.

Hunter, F. (1953) *Community Power Structure* Chapel Hill, NC., University of North Carolina Press.

ICPSR (1977) *The CPS 1976 American National Election Study:* vol. I *Introduction and Codebook,* vol. II *Notes, Frequencies, Addendum and Questionnaires* Ann Arbor, Mich., ICPSR.

Iremonger, L. (1970) *The Fiery Chariot: a Study of British Prime Ministers and the Search for Love* London, Secker & Warburg.

Jenkins, H. (1980) *Rank and File* London, Croom Helm.

Jenkins, R. (1968) *Mr Balfour's Poodle* (2nd edn) London, Collins

Kearns, D. (1976) *Lyndon Johnson and the American Dream* New York, NY., Harper & Row.

Kellner, P., and Crowther-Hunt, Lord, (1980) *The Civil Servants: An Inquiry into Britain's Ruling Class* London, Macdonald and Jane's.

Key, V. O. (1949) *Southern Politics in State and Nation* New York, NY., Alfred A. Knopf.

Key, V. O. (1955) 'A Theory of Critical Elections' *JP* XVII, 1, pp. 3-18.

Key, V. O. (1966) *The Responsible Electorate* Cambridge, Mass., Harvard UP.

Kirkpatrick, J. (1975) 'Representation in the American National Conventions: the case of 1972' *BJPS* V, 3, pp. 265-322.

Knight, J. (1974) *Northern Ireland: the Elections of 1973* London, The Arthur McDougall Fund.

Labour Party (1970) *Report of the 69th Annual Conference of the Labour Party, Blackpool 1970* London, Labour Party.

Laver, M. (1980) 'Political Solutions to the Collective Action Problem' *PS* XXVII, 2, pp. 195-209.

Laver, M. (1981) *The Politics of Private Desires* Harmondsworth, Penguin.

Lee, J. M. (1963) *Social Leaders and Public Persons: a Study of County Government in Cheshire since 1888* Oxford, Clarendon Press.

Lipset, S. M. (1960) *Political Man* London, Heinemann.

Lipset, S. M., and Rokkan, S. (1967) *Party Systems and Voter Alignments* New York, NY., Free Press.

McKenzie, R. T. (1964) *British Political Parties* (revised impression of 2nd edn) London, Heinemann.

McKenzie, R. T., and Silver, A. (1968) *Angels in Marble* London, Heinemann

Mackie, J. L. (1977) *Ethics: Inventing Right and Wrong* Harmondsworth, Penguin.

McLean, I. S. (1973) 'Oxford and Bridgwater' in C. Cook and J. Ramsden (eds) *By-elections in British Politics* London, Macmillan, pp. 140-64.

McLean, I. S. (1975) *Keir Hardie* London, Allen Lane

McLean, I. S. (1976) *Elections* London, Longman.

McLean, I. S. (1977) 'The Politics of Nationalism and Devolution', *PS* XXV, 3, pp. 425-430.

McLean, I. S. (1980) 'Party Organisation' in C. Cook and !. Taylor (eds) *The Labour Party* London, Longman, pp. 32-49.

McLean, I. S. (1981) 'The Social Contract in *Leviathan* and the Prisoners' Dilemma Supergame' *PS* XXIX, 3, pp. 339-51.

Marsh, A. (1977) *Protest and Political Consciousness* Beverly Hills, Calif. Sage.

Mayhew, D. R. (1974) *Congress: the electoral connection* New Haven, Conn., Yale UP.

Mill, J. S. (1972) *Utilitarianism, On Liberty* and *Considerations on Representative Government* (Everyman edn) London, Dent. (*On Liberty* originally published in 1859 and *Representative Government* in 1861).

Miller, W. L. (1977) *Electoral Dynamics in Britain since 1918* New York, NY., St Martins Press.

Miller, W. L. (1980) 'What was the Profit in Following the Crowd? the Effectiveness of Party Strategies on Immigration and Devolution' *BJPS* X, 1, pp. 15-38.

Miller, W. L. (1981) *The End of British Politics? Scots and English Political Behaviour in the Seventies* Oxford, Clarendon Press.

Mills, C. W. (1956) *The Power Elite* New York, NY., Oxford University Press.

Morison, S. E., Commager, H. S., and Leuchtenburg, W. E. (1969) *The Growth of the American Republic, vol. II.* (6th edn) New York, NY., Oxford University Press.

Mueller, D. C. (1979) *Public Choice* Cambridge, Cambridge UP.

Murray, B. K. (1980) *The People's Budget 1909-10: Lloyd George and Liberal Politics* Oxford, Clarendon Press.

Namier, (Sir) L. (1957) *The Structure of Politics at the Accession of George III* (2nd edn) London, Macmillan.

Nie, N. H., Verba, S., and Petrocik, J. R. (1979) *The Changing American Voter* (2nd edn) Cambridge, Mass., Harvard UP.

Niemi, R. G., and Weisberg, H. F., (eds) (1976) *Controversies in American Voting Behavior* San Francisco, Calif., W. H. Freeman & Co.

Niskanen, W. A. (1971) *Bureaucracy and Representative Government* Chicago, Ill., Aldine Publishing Co.

Niskanen, W. A. and others (1973) *Bureaucracy: Servant or Master?* London, IEA.

Nordlinger, E. (1967) *The Working-class Tories* London, Macgibbon & Kee.

Nozick, R. (1974) *Anarchy, State and Utopia* Oxford, Blackwell.

O'Brien, C. C. (1974) *States of Ireland* (2nd edn) St. Albans, Herts, Panther.

Office of the Lord President of the Council (1976) *Devolution: The English Dimension. A Consultative Document.* London, HMSO.

O'Leary, C. (1962) *The Elimination of Corrupt Practices in British Elections 1868-1911* Oxford, Clarendon Press.

Olson, M. (1965) *The Logic of Collective Action* Cambridge, Mass., Harvard UP.

Ostrogorski, M. (1902) *Democracy and the Organisation of Political Parties* vol I London, Macmillan.

Page, B. I. (1976) 'The Theory of Political Ambiguity', *APSR* LXX, 3, pp. 742-52.

Page, B. I. (1978) *Choices and Echoes in Presidential Elections: Rational Man and Electoral Democracy* Chicago, Ill., University of Chicago Press.

Pakenham, F. (1967) *Peace by Ordeal* (4th edn) London, New English Library.

Pelling, H. M. (1967) *Social Geography of British Elections 1885-1910* London, Macmillan.

Peters, R. S. (1967) *Hobbes* (2nd edn) Harmondsworth, Penguin.

Plott, C. (1976) 'Axiomatic Social Choice Theory', *AJPS,* XX, pp. 511-96.

Plowden, W. (1971) *The Motor-car and Politics 1896-1970* London, Bodley Head.

Plunkitt, G. W. (1963) *Plunkitt of Tammany Hall* (ed. by W. L. Riordon with an intro. by Arthur Mann) New York, NY., E. P. Dutton & Co. Originally published in 1905.

Pulzer, P. G. J. (1975) *Political Representation and Elections in Britain* (3rd edn) London, Allen & Unwin. Published in the USA as *Political Representation and Elections: Parties and Voting in Great Britain,* Praeger.

Ramsden, J. (1978) *The Age of Balfour and Baldwin 1902-40 (A History of the Conservative Party, vol. 3)* London, Longman.

Ranney, A. (1979) 'The Political Parties: Reform and Decline' in A. King (ed.) *The New American Political System* Washington, DC, AEI, pp. 213-47.

Rawls, J. (1972) *A Theory of Justice* Oxford, Clarendon Press.

Riker, W. H., and Ordeshook, P. (1973) *An Introduction to Positive Political Theory* Englewood Cliffs, NJ., Prentice-Hall.

Robertson, D. B. (1976) *A Theory of Party Competition* London, Wiley.

Rose, R. (1971) *Governing without Consensus; an Irish perspective* London, Faber & Faber.

Rose, R. (1976) *The Problem of Party Government* (2nd edn) Harmondsworth, Penguin.

Rose, R. (1980a) *Do Parties Make a Difference?* Chatham, NJ., Chatham House.

Rose, R. (1980b) *Politics in England* (3rd edn) London, Faber & Faber.

Sacks, P. M. (1976) *The Donegal Mafia: an Irish Political Machine* New Haven, Conn., Yale UP.

Sampson, A. (1962) *Anatomy of Britain* London, Hodder & Stoughton.

Scammon, R. and Wattenberg, B. (1970) *The Real Majority* New York, NY., Coward-McCann.

Schumpeter, J. (1954) *Capitalism, Socialism and Democracy* (4th British edn) London, Allen & Unwin. Originally published in 1942.

Sedgemore, B. (1980) *The Secret Constitution: An Analysis of the Political Establishment* London, Hodder and Stoughton.

Siegfried, A. (1913) *Tableau Politique de la France de l'Ouest sous la IIIe République* Paris, Armand Colin.

Snow, C. P. (1962) *Science and Government* (revised edn) New York, NY., Mentor.

Social and Community Planning Research (1973) *Devolution and other Aspects of Government: An Attitude Survey* (Royal Commission on the Constitution, Research paper no. 7) London, SCPR for the Office of Population Censuses and Surveys.

Steed, M. (1979) 'The United Kingdom -- What Components', Paper for the Political Studies Association Work Group on UK Politics, Warwick 1979.

Stimson, J. A. (1976) 'Belief Systems: Constraint, Complexity and the 1972 Election' in Niemi and Weisberg (1976), pp. 138-59.

Stokes, D. (1966) 'Spatial Models of Party Competition' in Campbell *et al.,* (1966), pp. 161-79.

Storr, A. (1969) 'The Man' in A. J. P. Taylor *et al., Churchill: Four Faces and the Man* London, Allen Lane, pp. 203-46.

Teer, F. and Spence, J. (1973) *Political Opinion Polls* London, Hutchinson.

Times, The (1980) *Times Guide to the House of Commons 1979* London, Times Books.

Titmuss, R. (1958) *Essays on 'the Welfare State'* London, Allen & Unwin.

Tucker, R. (1977) 'The Georges' Wilson Reexamined: An Essay on Psychobiography' *APSR* LXXI, 2, pp. 606-18.

Tufte, E. (1980) *Political Control of the Economy* (2nd edn) Princeton, NJ., Princeton UP.

Tullock, G. (1965) *The Politics of Bureaucracy* Washington, DC, Public Affairs Press.

US Bureau of the Census (1975) *Historical Statistics of the United States, Colonial Times to 1970* Washington, DC, Bureau of the Census.

US Bureau of the Census (1976) *Statistical Abstract of the United States* (97th edn) Washington, DC, US Bureau of the Census.

Vincent, J. (1967) *Pollbooks: How Victorians Voted* London, Cambridge UP.

Wallas, G. (1948) *Human Nature in Politics* London, Constable. Originally published in 1908.

Ware, A. (1979a) *The Logic of Party Democracy* London, Macmillan.

Ware, A. (1979b) 'The End of Party Politics? Activist -- Office -- Seeker Relationships in the Colorado Democratic Party' *BJPS* IX, 2, pp. 237-50.

Ware, A. (1981) 'The 1980 US Elections' *PA* XXXIV, 2, pp. 174-90.

Whiteley, P. and Gordon, I. (1980) 'Middle class, Militant and Male' *New Statesman* 11 January 1980.

Wicksell, K. (1958) 'A New Principle of Just Taxation' in R. A. Musgrave and A. T. Peacock (eds) *Classics in the Theory of Public Finance* London, Macmillan, pp. 72-118.

Wilson, J. Q. (1974) 'The Politics of Regulation' in J. W. McKie (ed.) *Social Responsibility and the Business Predicament* Washington, DC, The Brookings Institution, pp. 135-68.

Wilson, J. Q. (1980) *American Government: Institutions and Policies* Lexington, Mass., D. C. Heath & Co.

Index